JOURNEY

FROM THE

LAND of NO

A GIRLHOOD

CAUGHT IN

REVOLUTIONARY

IRAN

JOURNEY

FROM THE

LAND OF NO

ROYA HAKAKIAN

CROWN PUBLISHERS
NEW YORK

Grateful acknowledgment is made to Farrar, Straus and Giroux, LLC, and Faber and Faber Ltd. for permission to reprint "Personal Helicon" from *The Opened Ground: Selected Poems 1966–1998* by Seamus Heaney. Copyright © 1998 by Seamus Heaney. British edition titled *New Selected Poems 1966–1987*. Reprinted by permission of Farrar, Straus and Giroux, LLC, and Faber and Faber Ltd.

Some of the names and identifying characteristics of the people described herein have been changed.

Published by Crown Publishers, New York, New York.
Member of the Crown Publishing Group, a division of Random House, Inc.
www.crownpublishing.com

CROWN is a trademark and the Crown colophon is a registered trademark of Random House, Inc.

Printed in the United States of America

DESIGN BY ELINA D. NUDELMAN

Library of Congress Cataloging-in-Publication Data
Hakakian, Roya.
Journey from the land of no : a girlhood caught in revolutionary Iran / Roya Hakakian.—1st. ed.
1. Hakakian, Roya.   2. Iranian American women—Biography.   3. Authors, Persian—Biography.   4. Political refugees—United States—Biography.
5. Iran—History—Revolution, 1979.   I. Title.
E184.I5H35   2006
955.05'3'092—dc22   2003021662

ISBN 1-4000-4611-4

10 9 8 7 6 5 4 3 2 1

First Edition

BETWEEN 1982 AND 1990 AN UNKNOWN NUMBER OF
IRANIAN WOMEN POLITICAL PRISONERS WERE RAPED ON THE
EVE OF THEIR EXECUTIONS BY GUARDS WHO ALLEGED THAT
KILLING A VIRGIN WAS A SIN IN ISLAM.

———— ≝✦≝ ————

This book is dedicated to the memory of those women.

As a child, they could not keep me from wells
And old pumps with buckets and windlasses.
I loved the dark drop, the trapped sky, the smells
Of waterweed, fungus and dank moss.

One, in a brickyard, with a rotted board top.
I savoured the rich crash when a bucket
Plummeted down at the end of a rope.
So deep you saw no reflection in it.

A shallow one under a dry stone ditch
Fructified like any aquarium.
When you dragged out long roots from the soft mulch
A white face hovered over the bottom.

Others had echoes, gave back your own call
With a clean new music in it. And one
Was scaresome, for there, out of ferns and tall
Foxgloves, a rat slapped across my reflection.

Now, to pry into roots, to finger slime,
To stare, big-eyed Narcissus, into some spring
Is beneath all adult dignity. I rhyme
To see myself, to set the darkness echoing.

——PERSONAL HELICON, Seamus Heaney

God is not only a gentleman and a sport, he is a Kentuckian too.

——THE SOUND AND THE FURY, William Faulkner

CONTENTS

HISTORICAL NOTE   5

1
NEW YORK CITY, JULY 13, 1999   9

2
THE LITTLE BLACK FISH   19

3
THE BABY BLUE BMW   44

4
FARAH   67

CONTENTS

5

ON THE ROOFTOPS   *90*

6

THE BIG BANG   *114*

7

FRESH AIR, SINGING DOVES, BUDDING FLOWERS,
SASHAYING SPRING, AND OTHER
POSTREVOLUTIONARY MIRACLES   *140*

8

THE DREAMERS   *170*

9

1984   *196*

EPILOGUE   *230*

GLOSSARY OF TERMS   *234*

CHRONOLOGY   *237*

ACKNOWLEDGMENTS   *244*

JOURNEY

FROM THE

LAND OF NO

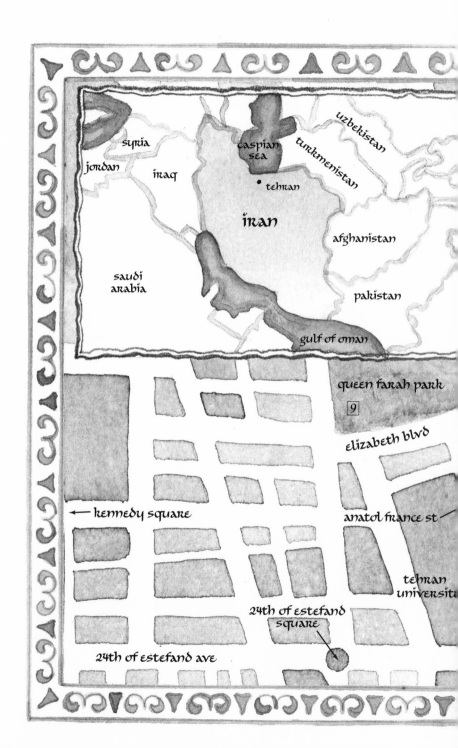

tehran 1978

1	Victoria Hotel
2	Polidor Cinema
3	Embassy of Iraq
4	Pahlavi Foundation
5	Blossom & Nightingale Ice Cream Parlor
6	Negeen Confectioners
7	City Theater
8	Embassy of Israel
9	Museum
10	Nelson Pharmacy
11	Coral High School for Girls
12	Hashtroodi High School for Boys

1

2

crown prince square

alley of the distinguished

minoo alley

10

3

saba st

11

4

damascus st

5

6

12

palace square

persepolis st

7

8

crown prince park

palace ave

pahlavi ave

hafez st

HISTORICAL NOTE

IN DECEMBER 1977, PRESIDENT JIMMY CARTER TOASTED Mohammad Reza Shah Pahlavi, the king of Iran, at a royal dinner in Tehran with the following words: "Iran, because of the leadership of the shah, is an island of stability in one of the most troubled areas of the world."

There indeed was an Iran perfectly at peace and on its way to a great future. The nation's annual growth rate was roughly double the average of other third world countries, and per capita income was on the rise; so were student population and life expectancy. Education and health had improved. The infant mortality rate, malnutrition, endemic diseases, and illiteracy had been reduced.

But there was another Iran, too, where individual and civil liberties lagged behind health and economic growth, where political parties, except that of the shah, were banned, and where freedom of expression did not exist. The shah wanted to restore the glory of ancient Persia to twentieth-century Iran, yet contrary to his grand aspiration, his intelligence service, SAVAK, hounded writers, intellectuals, and political activists and tortured them in prisons. In time SAVAK became the major source of discontent among the educated class.

And yet not all reasons for the dissatisfaction with the Pahlavi regime were rooted within Iran's realities. Living just to the south of the Soviet Union, Iranian intellectuals had been inspired by its early revolutionary history and utopian spirit. In the global cold war, the majority of secular, educated Iranians stood against imperialism, which the United States represented for them. And in 1978, when those intellectuals heard the fiery rhetoric of a clergyman, they answered his call. From the humblest of settings, exiled in France, Ayatollah Khomeini vowed to stand against the tyranny of monarchy and of the United States, which he denounced for undermining Iran's sovereignty. He had emphasized over and over that he had no desire to be in power, only to return to his native, holy city of Qom and continue his religious studies.

When he finally arrived in Iran on February 1, 1979, days after the departure of the shah, he returned as a leader who had unified the Left and the Right, and galvanized millions to demand an end to 2,500 years of monarchy. Those millions also included hundreds of young Jews. Against the wishes of their elders, many Jewish students joined the revolution, hoping to recast their identities as secular Iranians, who would then assimilate seamlessly into the fabric of the utopia the revolution promised.

On February 12, 1979, Ayatollah Khomeini's sacred status rose to that of an "imam," only a step away from the prophet's in the Shiite tradition. He declared the definitive victory of the revolution. By April an overwhelming majority of Iranians voted for the establishment of an Islamic republic.

Within weeks, Khomeini moved from Qom to the capital, Tehran, to personally lead the nation's transition to the new social order. By the end of the second year, he had broken nearly every promise he had made. Every underground group that had joined a coalition with him to overthrow the shah was banned again. The control of all civil and political facets of life fell into the hands of a group of young radicals who called themselves members of Hezbollah, Party of God.

The 100,000-member Jewish community of Iran, the second largest community of Jews in the Middle East, after Israel, fell into disarray. The new regime's pronunciation of Israel as Iran's greatest enemy reawakened anti-Semitic sentiments. Though in several major speeches Ayatollah Khomeini recognized the Iranian Jewish community as belonging to the people that the holy Koran viewed as legitimate "people of the book," the social, economic, and educational opportunities of Jews were fast dwindling. They began to emigrate from Iran, a country in which their history preceded that of Muslims by several hundred years.

Women suffered an even greater loss of opportunities. Appearing in public without the veil became unlawful. And the new Islamic dress code, consisting of a headdress, long, loose overcoat, and pants, was implemented shortly after the victory of the revolution. Women lost the right to divorce. Abortion was declared illegal. And most engineering fields as well as law schools refused to accept female students. By September 1980 the world had enforced severe sanctions on Iran to condemn the seizure of the American embassy in Tehran and the taking of fifty-two American diplomats hostage. That September, Saddam Hussein declared war against Iran. Doom overtook Iran, and its most telling sign was the exchange rate. In 1978 seventy rials were exchanged for one dollar. By 1984 the figure had shot past ten thousand rials.

It took some time for the clerics to solidify their hold on power, and for Iran to reach that state of despair. But in the interim, the country, especially Tehran, experienced a period of unparalleled freedom. For those who lived in Tehran, that brief period following the revolution remains the most memorable time of their lives. History books speak of the Iranian revolution as one of the greatest revolutions, even the last great revolution, of the twentieth century. The revolution was that and more. For the children of that era, 1979 was not only a year but also a love affair, the most alluring love of their lives. In time, it proved to be the cruelest, too.

This is the story of that affair.

1

NEW YORK CITY, JULY 13, 1999

IT WAS AN ORDINARY MORNING AT THE OFFICE. WRAPPED in a heavy sweater, sleeves pulled over fingers hiding from the arctic indoor summer temperatures, I had every reason to expect this to be a day like any other. CNN was on. A pile of several major dailies lay on one side of my desk, and on the other was a second stack of magazines I had brought back from the Delta Shuttle courtesy stand. The first order of business was to answer e-mails, which I usually managed to do while sipping a tall cup of latté. I glanced at the names in the in-box, keeping an eye out for any breaking news on the Associated Press wire service. The telephone rang.

"Roya speaking."

"Hi, Roya. This is David, David Unger, calling from the *New York Times.*"

"Oh, hi! You are . . ."

"An editorial writer working on a piece on the recent student uprisings in Iran. You come highly recommended as a source. Is this a good time?"

No. It was not a good time. It was never a good time to talk about Iran. I rarely did. But this call, I knew, I had to take. Thousands of students had taken to the streets in the largest pro-reform demonstration since 1979. Now, in the demonstration's third day, the students were calling on the newly elected president, Mohammad Khatami, to join their movement against the "hardline" elements in power, mainly the supreme leader, Seyed Ali Khamenei. Many had been arrested. A few had disappeared, among them Elahe, a dear friend. And sitting in my office, watching the news, seeing young men and women face the riot police, their shirts bloodied, their faces hidden under rags, thugs charging at them with batons, seeing them be clubbed and fall to the pavement, was all too familiar. All too frustrating. There was nothing I could do to help them or my missing friend, except to talk to an editorialist. In my guilty helplessness, I had placed all hope in the *New York Times* to save Elahe, the students, and Iran itself in a sharp cluster of five hundred words or less. So I said, "Yes. I have been expecting your call. But hold on for just a minute, please."

This was simply a call between a television journalist and her colleague in print. Still, I got up from my chair, peeked into the hallway, and quietly shut my door. This was a call about Iran; no call could be more personal. We began talking.

I had expected to hear from David. I had also expected the conversation to proceed as it often does with Americans. They come, I had decided, in two kinds: the misinformed, who think of Iran as a backward nation of Arabs, veiled and turbaned, living on the periphery of oases and fairly represented by a government of mullahs; and the misguided, who believed the shah's regime was a puppet government run by the CIA, and who think that Ayatollah Khomeini and his clerical cabal are an authentic, home-grown answer to unwarranted U.S. meddling.

The first group always amused me. In their company, I would blame every appalling trait in my character on my "Bedouin upbringing." Walking along Coney Island beach on a hot summer evening, I licked the drops of ice cream off my palms, and when I saw the shocked look on my date's face, I explained that my lack of etiquette was due to a childhood spent in a land where napkins and utensils were unheard of. His believing blue eyes welled with tears of empathy.

A college roommate once asked what my family used for transportation in Tehran. I told her we kept six camels of various sizes in our backyard. My father rode the papa camel, my mother the mama camel, my brothers the younger camels, and I the baby camel. While my roommate's common sense was still in the grip of political correctness, I went on to design a fantastically intricate grid of four-legged traffic regulations for bovines on even days and equines on odd.

But that second group—those misguided Americans—exasperated me. Bright individuals abandoned inquiry and resorted to obsolete formulas: America had done Iran wrong. Therefore the clerics cut ties with the United States. Therefore the clerics were leading the nation to sovereignty. These individuals had yet to realize that though Iran's rulers fervently opposed U.S. imperialism, they were neither just to nor loved by their own people. This second group had not accepted the notion that the enemy of their enemy was yet another enemy.

It took only one question for me to decide that David belonged to the second group. He asked, "Do the 'reformists,' backed by President Khatami, stand a chance against the 'hard-liners'?"

This bipolar division between reformists and hard-liners was as crude as my own division between misinformed and misguided Americans. Reducing a nation of seventy million, with three thousand years of history, to two simple camps infuriated me. The assumption that Iran was on the verge of an imminent transformation if only one faction managed to subdue the other had the ring of a sensational headline, and though as a reporter I understood its logic, as an Iranian I detested it. True watchers of Iran knew that Iran itself was the "beloved" its great poets had serenaded for centuries: capricious yet slow, inspiring hope in one breath and evoking despair in another.

However, David quickly added that the editorials did not always reflect his own personal views. In fact, they often did not. This was an important disclaimer. Several more nuanced questions followed. His voice was tender. If a deadline was looming, his voice did not reveal it. In its timbre, there was time and infinite patience, which encouraged me to tell him my worst fears. Every horrifying possibility flashed through my mind: Elahe assaulted, bleeding in a ditch or along one of the many canals of Tehran; or sitting before interrogators, blindfolded, forced to write a recantation letter. Talking to David, I dressed in words the horrors I was conjuring. I told him so. I also told him that I had no faith in the new president, or any other cleric, to deliver what the students were demanding. I saw that the protestors were in grave danger. In the most dignified way I knew, I begged him to write with utmost urgency.

The next day brought an editorial headlined FATEFUL MOMENT IN IRAN; the next week, the quashing of the uprising; the third week, the news of Elahe and her release from custody; the next month, another e-mail from David—a new editorial deadline.

In the weeks that followed, David's notes continued to arrive. He wanted to know about the reformists' background and their former allegiance; the Iranian relationship with the Lebanese Hezbollah; the role of secular Iranians in the revolution of 1979 and in the subsequent fallout. With Elahe's release, I had little incentive to talk about Iran. Writing to David took real effort. I had to provide him with the "insider facts," information only natives are privy to, and add my own views, which were embittered by my history. Every time I wanted to substantiate an opinion, I drew upon a personal experience I had never talked about before, until at last I wrote, apologetically, that I could not continue. Despite my reputation, I confessed that I was not a good source after all. There were experts far better than I, whose names I suggested. When it came to Iran, I admitted, I was anything but objective. The past and the events of the years that followed the revolution had biased me forever.

Within moments after I e-mailed him the note I thought would be the end of all notes between us, a sharp beep announced the arrival of a new e-mail.

From: David@Nytimes.com

To: RDH@cbsnews.com

Subject: The years that followed the revolution.

r,

Tell me about them.

d

When you have been a refugee, abandoned all your loves and belongings, your memories become your belongings. Images of the past, snippets of old conversations, furnish the world within your mind. When you have nothing left to guard, you guard your memories. You guard them with silence. You do not draw your treasures into the light, lest exposure soften their sharp—sad or gay—details (the best lesson I ever learned from visiting museums). Remembering becomes not simply a preoccupation but a full-time occupation. What you once witnessed is the story that brought journalists to your doorstep, but they left without the scoop. What you once witnessed is what scholars sought in the archives but did not find. What you once witnessed is what biographers intended to write. But how much can biographers do if the witnesses are silent?

When you belong to a breed on the verge of extinction, a Jewish woman from the Islamic Republic of Iran living in the United States, one small slip can turn you into a poster child for someone else's crusade. And you know of nothing more suspect than a crusade. Memory is the membrane in which the past is sealed and also the blueprint of what you once, when you were at your most clearheaded, envisioned as the future. You keep silent. To guard all that, true. But also because you cannot tell pain from anger. And since you do not wish to displace them onto an innocent listener, you do not allow yourself pain or anger. You walk on. You must walk on. In the new country, you must begin anew. To make yourself do so, you invent a metaphor. Not a beautiful metaphor, but a practical one to propel you. You imagine you are a secondhand car whose odometer has been reset to zero by exile, that craftiest of dealers. With all the old parts, you are recast as a brand-new human engine. Within you is all the clanking, hissing, and racket of past rides. But you muffle it all and press on.

David wanted me to speak. But he had no crusade. A historian, he was looking for what he knew was still too soon to have been written. He was a voice without a face. Somewhere on the top floor of another New York City high-rise he sat behind a desk. I had never seen him. All I knew of him was the words that kept arriving. Our friendship had been formed in written words, the only life those memories could have if they ever were to be expressed. And in English. To write about Iran in Persian would be daunting. Instead of reexamining the memories, I feared that in Persian, I might begin to relive them. Persian could summon the teenager at sea. English sheltered the adult survivor, safely inside a lighthouse. I did not know how to use the language of the censors to speak against them; to use the very language by which I had been denied so much as a Jew, a woman, a secular citizen, and a young poet. The love of Iran was still in my heart, yet I could not return. The irrevocable journey I had made was not the physical one, out of Iran. It was the journey from "no," from the perpetual denials. And what I had painstakingly arrived at, greater than even the new land, was a new language, the vessel of my flight to vast possibilities.

I postponed writing David till I could be certain I wanted to commit myself to telling him. His notes had opened the floodgates, and a world once shut away had come rushing back at me. But how and where would I begin? In need of a reprieve, I accepted a reporting assignment that took me to Albany, Georgia, for a few days.

The Reverend Jerry Cochran had served in the U.S. Navy in the early 1970s and was suffering from a lung disease. Like most African Americans of his generation, Jerry had been assigned the most undesirable tasks while in the navy, among them the scraping of the nonskid coating off the deck of the USS *Enterprise*. Within two years, Jerry had been diagnosed with a "respiratory disease of unknown origin" and discharged. He believed the disease had resulted from the polluted air he had inhaled while working on the deck. Now a biopsy proved the presence of elements, identical to those within the coating he had once scraped, in his chest. The dust was gradually hardening Jerry's lung tissue and lessening his breathing capacity. Jerry was slowly suffocating.

Driving past the cotton fields in rural Georgia, I mulled over the many details that demanded my attention: the few unclear facts, the original documents, footage to shoot, sounds to record, his difficulty breathing and speaking, his wheezing. I decided to arrive at Jerry's church early, to soak in my surroundings, an old habit that had got me far as a child. I reviewed all the questions and went over what I needed to prepare for the crew and our correspondent before the on-camera interviews. This was a man on the brink of death, I thought. He was about to trust his final words to me. And it was up to me to show how he had been mistreated and misdiagnosed and as a result was dying.

Inside the church, rows of children sat around tables, doing homework. Mrs. Cochran welcomed me. She asked if I was too tired or had had any trouble finding my way. The after-school hours were the busiest at the church, she explained, and she apologized for the noisy surroundings. But I insisted on watching the children and staff go about their business. For reasons I never understood, I have always felt instantly at ease among black

Americans and forget my own outsiderness. I said, "I'm happy to wait here and watch the kids. The reverend must be busy. I know I've come early."

"The reverend has been on pins and needles for days waiting for you," she replied, sounding like an exhausted wife who has had to contend with far too much for far too long. "It's not every day *60 Minutes* comes to our neighborhood."

To find a quieter location for the filming, Mrs. Cochran took me on a tour of the building. We walked past several rooms, each filled to the ceiling with boxes of evidence the reverend had gathered on his own condition and that of his fellow servicemen. Years of correspondence had amounted to pile after pile of documents: letters from the Veterans Administration, the U.S. Navy, the Occupational Safety and Health Administration, the Environmental Protection Agency, and on and on. Some bore the stamps of the White House, others of the U.S. Congress. Behind the facade of an unassuming two-story structure hid a colossal archive. And at the end of its last corridor, I imagined a gaunt man on his deathbed.

But I was wrong. In the last room, at the end of a hallway, behind a desk, in a suit, sat a corpulent man, who rose exuberantly to his feet and greeted me. He looked hale and cheerful. Upon seeing the buoyant reverend, I felt the worst of a journalist's fears rush over me: I was chasing a sham.

It took hours to pore over papers and sift through medical reports till I found the documentary evidence that attested to the severity of Jerry's condition. But more compelling than the records were his testimonies. At first, when he saw the skeptical expression on my face, he slapped his chest and said, as if before a judge, that his heart could no longer bear the weight of a history denied. The disease in those boxes, he pleaded, would kill him faster than the disease in his lungs. He laid out photographs, exhibits for a jury of one, of himself and his buddies, their arms on one another's shoulders, their faces bright with the proud smiles of young, invincible men, standing in uniforms against the majestic background of the sea. They dreamed of serving their country and hoped for a great future. But the dust had buried their dreams. Two of those young men were dead. Being forgotten had already killed their spirits. The dust would finish the rest.

Jerry's eyes fixed on my face as if expecting a confession. He asked whether I understood what it meant to be bearing a story never told. "I do," I said with a voice on the brink of breaking. He paused, examined my expression, and, seeing that he had won me over, lowered himself into a chair, to rest at last.

Back at the hotel, long past midnight, tossing in my bed, I was restless to write. The feel of Jerry's firm grip as we shook hands still enveloped my hand, and his opening line kept playing in my mind: "I have waited years for you to come and hear my story." So he had begun.

And so I began.

2

THE LITTLE BLACK FISH

Once upon a time there was a little black fish who lived with his mother in a stream that gushed out of the crack of a rock and flowed into a ravine. At night, the two slept under a roof of moss and the little fish dreamed, if only once, to see moonlight spread along their beds. All day long, he and his mother went up and down, up and down, up and down the narrow path of the stream, crammed among a crowd of neighbors. And lately, he had lost all enthusiasm for these boring outings and was wondering just how to tell his mother about it.

MY BROTHER JAVID READ TO ME. WITH ONE HAND, HE HELD the book; with the other, he brushed the bangs out of my eyes.

"Shut a book first, before you shut your eyes," he pulled my head back and said to my face.

"Yes," I replied obediently, though we both knew it was a promise I could never keep. He read to me so my last thoughts at night would be great thoughts. I listened so that I could be awash with great sensations. I laid my head in his lap: his palm on my forehead, my cheek against his thigh, the plush pile of the rug under my torso, and the cool courtyard tiles beneath my legs. Soon after "Once upon time," I closed my eyes. One by one, my fingers slid into the grooves between the tiles and locked into them. I was blind to the world around me, touched by all things dear—this was how the stories came to life. This was how I listened best.

The grooves! They were the secret scale by which I measured my growth. The adults had their own fancy scales. But I trusted the grooves. And in that summer of 1975, when my fingers finally outgrew them, I knew that my "little Roya" years were finally over. But the point was hard to argue when the official calendar, the proof of all proofs, still declared me nine.

The tiles, sixty-eight of them from the front door to the building, thirty from wall to wall, were also the records of our family life. When I ran through the courtyard, each indentation under my bare feet evoked a different memory in my mind. Near row eight, I had tripped over the garden hose and chipped a tooth. Around rows sixteen and seventeen, where the tiles were mislaid and the groove lines did not match up, Father had let go of the back of my bicycle and I balanced myself without him. At row fifty, the site of a dozen banged knees, the scalloped edge of our fountain loomed. On its surface, juniper berries fell during the late afternoons when Father watered the garden.

Shooting past the tops of the walls that delineated all the homes, our junipers oriented passersby. Lost visitors asking for directions were guided to turn at the alley's corner, where the second most eye-catching landmark was the gold Jewish prayer ornament nailed askew on the frame of a set of blue iron doors. But the first was the junipers behind those doors. And so the whole neighborhood directed traffic of all kinds toward or away from our trees. They gave the neighborhood its distinction, my family contended. If the quibble ever rose among the neighbors, and it often did, as to just why the alley had a name as grand as the Alley of the Distinguished, we proclaimed that in all of Tehran only one house had junipers so tall that their pinnacles came into view only when the viewer's neck, as I had coined, "reached the point of ouch!" And that house was number three in no alley other than the Alley of the Distinguished in the fourteenth postal district. "One" stood for God. "Two" stood for the country's beloved shah and his queen. But "three" stood for the house with the magnificent junipers, the Hakakian house. On the subject of which courtyard had the most fragrant honeysuckle, whose wintersweet bloomed earliest, whose flowerbeds had the most colorful arrangement of pansies, whose imperial roses were the most velvety, or whose gooseberry tree cast the widest shade in the afternoons, though we had the best of each, we were willing to concede to our neighbors. But not on the junipers. They blessed the neighborhood. And anyone who disagreed had to spar with one of the city's most persuasive public speakers, with Father. He believed that we owed everything to the junipers, whose cool breeze brought us relief on hot summer nights. And on sunny days, it was in the emerald frame of the junipers that the shimmering, two-story facade of crushed glass and white cement of our house lodged itself.

This spirit of modesty, which Father extended to all people and objects about us, was ultimately captured by him in a couplet etched in calligraphy and hung above our hallway door:

THE HAKAKIANS' IS A HOME OF DERVISHES
WITHOUT A CARE FOR THE WORLD'S RICHES
NO ONE'S A STRANGER IN OUR HOME
EVERYONE'S FAMILY UNDER OUR DOME

Days after he composed that poem, many of our friends and neighbors inserted their own family names in place of Hakakian and hung the poem above their doors. Unperturbed by the piracy, Father reveled in the sensation his little verse had caused and promised, "There is more where that came from!"

There was indeed, and it usually came on Friday afternoons, when he would sit on the floor of his study, the same room as our living room, which turned into his and Mother's bedroom at night. In his lap he laid a notepad and stared, unseeingly, at the courtyard. For those few hours, he allowed nothing to distract him. If Mother asked what he wanted for dinner, without shifting his gaze, he murmured, "Bread and yogurt," which meant he had not heard her at all. His gaze remained fixed till a faint smile formed on his lips. And instantly, his glasses slid from his forehead down to the ridge of his nose: a line was jotted. Resting his glasses back on his forehead, he looked into the distance once more, rubbing his thumb against his fingers, as if to firm his grip on an elusive word or a fleeting thought. And when he had it, the glasses slid down once more: a new line was born. There he sat content, caught in the traffic of a pair of glasses, captivated by the steering of his own pen. Watching him, I prayed to someday be on the same road, peeking at the same world.

―•― ≣♦≣ ―•―

One day, the little black fish finally told his mother, "I want to go and find the end of this stream. I think about it so much that I cannot sleep at night. I want to know what is happening in other places." But his mother only laughed and said, "What end? What other places? This stream is all there is to all the waters. We were born here and we will die here." But the little black fish was at his wit's end and could do nothing other than be bold and persist: "Mother, the day has an end, the night has an end, the week has an end—so, too, this stream must have an end. If I do not go, I will never be happy here."

―•― ≣♦≣ ―•―

Javid shook his leg to see if I was awake, but I pressed my eyelids together, knowing that he would then whisper, "Is dream dreaming?" That was what I wanted to hear, a question that could be put to me and no one else, for *I* was the family's Roya, Persian for "dream," their one and only dream.

Nine years earlier, on a bright October day, Father had stood in front of a schoolyard of hundreds of students, administering the morning prayers, when his assistant tapped him on the shoulder and said in his ear, "Mr. Hakakian, thanks be to God, the hospital nurse telephoned. Your wife just delivered. She and the baby are both fine."

"What is the baby?"

"What did you ask God to give you?"

"I already have three boys. I dearly hoped for a girl."

"God always grants the wishes of the pious."

And there, before rows of his single-file pupils, Father announced that he had just had a baby girl and his dream had come true, and he vowed to call me just that. It was a decision about which he felt more confident every time he heard of my smallest achievements. He would smile, nod like a sage whose foresight had proven true, tell and retell his favorite story:

"Helen and I, along with Roya, were coming home from a visit to my sister. Her husband, Yehouda, had just returned from Israel and brought me a pair of leather Jaguar-brand shoes. I had wanted a pair of Jaguars for so long. When he gave them to me, I clutched the bag to my chest and didn't let go all evening. But in the taxi, I put the bag down and somehow forgot about it. We got out, and the moment the taxi took off, I said, 'My shoes! I left them in the taxi.' Suddenly Roya, with those reedy legs of hers, started running up Pahlavi Avenue, so lithely, you'd think she were a gazelle. She ran, unfazed by cars or pedestrians. Her mother and I stood watching until she nearly disappeared among the cars at Crown Prince Square. My heart was pounding with worry until she reappeared, running in the dark toward us, flashing a triumphant smile, waving the bag in the air. I knew that night those reedy legs of hers would take her far in life. Mark my words: She's a dream that will come true!"

What already was true was the dreaminess of our summer evenings together as a family. With Javid's voice in my ear, I stretched out lazily while life buzzed around me in the courtyard, where my youngest brother, Behzad, read Nikolai Gogol's *Taras Bulba*. Even on the quietest evenings, the rustle of juniper leaves, the hum of our two fluorescent lights, and the rush of pencil on the pages of the sketchbook of my oldest brother, Albert, could be heard. It was nothing spectacular that made our bliss spectacularly complete: Mother only had to arrive with a tray of tea and a bowl of scooped honeydew melon. Seeing her, Father put away the hose and washed his hands as water poured on his enormous bare feet. He threw a fistful of water on his broad forehead and slid a hand over his thinning gray hair, to make the most of a single splash. Then he turned on the fountain, and instantly the goldfish swam to the surface. Under the flow, the colored glass fragments in the pool's bed glimmered. He sat next to Mother, raised his tea glass, and examined its hue: too pale a yellow and he groaned that his tea had seen a policeman and lost its blush to fear; too deep a yellow and he wondered if it had been overbrewed. Then he threw a sugar cube up into the air, caught it with his lips, and drank anyway. With the cube between his teeth, he lisped to Mother, "This tea tastes excellent, Mrs. Helen." He uttered the "Mrs." while assuming his courtliest look, stretching his long neck, looking at Mother from the corners of his eyes, as if at his bejeweled queen, thus circuitously appointing himself king.

All the Hakakians claimed a bit of royalty, though our case hinged entirely on proximity. Number three Alley of the Distinguished was located across from the Pahlavi Foundation, headquarters for the royal family's charity organization, in the heart of a trendy neighborhood. Just to the south of the pastoral Elizabeth Boulevard, our neighborhood had all the charm of the countryside, and because it was to the east of the city's bustling artery, Pahlavi Avenue, it also had all the vibrations of a metropolis. Where the boulevard crossed the avenue, Crown Prince Square stood. I was always aware of the presence of water murmuring in the canals along the sidewalks of all streets. But only at Crown Prince Square did the sound give way to a roaring vision: a grand fountain surrounded by several smaller ones, all in a ring of Iranian flags. When I beheld this view, a parent on each arm, everything I loved was in sight: family beside, Iran soaring above, water cascading ahead.

Crown Prince Square was also home to the very best a city could offer. For tourists looking for that postcard backdrop, there was a gigantic solar clock whose hands moved to a different sliver of flowers at every hour in springtime. For discriminating urbanites, the Polidor Cinema screened the latest foreign films. For the melancholic, a walk past the square pool, along the boulevard's canal, under the shade of its plane trees, was just what the doctor ordered. North of the square, row after row of boutiques lured the most sophisticated shoppers. And for the sweet-toothed, for me, Blossom and Nightingale ice-cream parlor, to the south of the square, only two blocks away from Negeen Confectioners, suffused the air with the smell of heaven. And this heavenly scent came from the building that faced the Pahlavi Foundation's main entrance. The foundation's second entrance opened onto Saba Street, which crossed our alley. At that intersection the imperial edifice nested itself, in eyeshot of number three.

The Pahlavi Foundation was a marble fortress behind wrought-iron gates. Its grounds were guarded twenty-four hours a day. The daytime patrol at the Saba Street entrance, the Corpulent Cop, a nickname he had grown fond of, sluggishly paced the length of the gate and twirled his baton each time he reached one end, almost out of breath. This paltry vigilance abated by noon. As the wind carried the smell of Mother's cooking, he found an excuse to ring our doorbell. Eager to feed mankind, Mother rushed to the door with a lunchbox. Seeing it, he registered a look of surprise day after day, and as tradition dictated, insisted on refusing her generosity, until she had begged him enough to accept.

Mother's kindness was returned not to her but to me, a perfectly undeserving beneficiary. Once a week, the Corpulent Cop snuck me inside the foundation. He stood outside the gates, fidgeting, giving me an occasional anxious look, as I entered the grounds. Left to the pristine marble arena, I mounted my bicycle and began to glide across the gray floor. Each lap added to my boldness. I took a hand off the handlebars. The thought of being the only one accelerating my bicycle on those divine premises thrilled me. The breeze whispered in my ears. Through the rods of the gates, the cars, lights, and people orbited around me. Speed intoxicated me. The stone busts of the king and the queen, still in awe, watched the nation's youngest champion, the inventor of bike-skating. Round and round. Another hand came off the handlebars. Round and round and round. Slowly I rose from the seat to stand on the pedals. By then, the Corpulent Cop, made nervous by my flamboyance, blew his whistle and pointed his baton at the NO ENTRY sign. A crash followed. So many laws and bones were broken for the sake of those lunchboxes. Laws, I learned early on, were the easiest things to break in Iran.

To Mother, the Corpulent Cop was "eternally indebted," but to Father, he was wholly reverential. When he saw the 8341 Tehran-T plate of Father's car turning the corner, he clicked his heels and beamed his bloated smile. He stood at attention, and the moment

Father stopped to salute him, the Corpulent Cop shouted, "At your service, Mr. Lieutenant!" Father's army stories had made the rounds and the Corpulent Cop was impressed by them. Two years in Fakkeh, a godforsaken southern border town between Iran and Iraq, fighting opium traffickers, was not the kind of inconvenience the Corpulent Cop ever subjected himself to. But he admired it in Father. Though he paced the royal gates, his admiration for Father together with his appetite for Mother's cooking had him watching our house more closely than the Pahlavi property.

In his deference to Father, the Corpulent Cop was not alone. When Father sauntered down the street, his hands clasped behind him, chest forward, always in a suit and tie even if he was only going to the corner grocery, perfect strangers felt compelled to acknowledge him with the only term of reverence they could bestow on a regal passerby: "Mr. Haji, good day!" Haji: a fellow Muslim fortunate enough to have been to Mecca. And my obliging father, in turn, said as he passed them, "May Allah keep you safe!" Not Khoda, Persian for God. No. Father invoked the Koranic equivalent to express his appreciation for living at a time and in a city where a Jew could mingle with others so freely that he was mistaken for a Muslim.

And among Jews, he received an even warmer reception. He earned 60,000 rials a month as a headmaster, roughly $900. But the community subsidized that figure by paying him respect. The missing zeroes on his paychecks bubbled at the bottom of the champagne glasses the guests raised to toast him after he declaimed a poem in honor of the bride and groom. When he put his right hand over his chest, lowering his head in their direction, he was still taller than most in attendance. Soon after he had made a speech, the unofficial seal of every matrimony, a tipsy father of the bride or groom grabbed the microphone from the wedding singer to make an important announcement. *Silence, please!* "The presence of Mr. Hakakian, the poet, the conscience of the community, and the tireless educator, ladies and gentlemen, blesses every couple's future. So may his shadow linger over the heads of his children and the community for one hundred and twenty years." A chorus of amens followed. At circumcision ceremonies, the howling baby was passed to Father to be soothed. The baby's tearful mother, touched by the solace her boy took in Father's attention, pledged to send him to study under Father's supervision and pleaded that he do to her child as he saw fit, beat him if necessary, for Mr. Hakakian could do no wrong. Then two ardent hands grabbed his face to seal his cheek with a reddish shade of sincerity and whisper to him, "See my boy as one of your own."

Being one of Father's own was an honor and a burden. People saw us as his ambassadors and expected us to show just the right blend of faith, intellect, and mastery of rhetoric, especially the ability to rhyme on demand. Each compliment showered on us, in reality, was an expectation indirectly declared. As the youngest Hakakian and the only girl, I inspired little hope and drew prayers to reverse my precociousness: *Inshallah,* God willing! My brother Bez, who was five years my senior and born in the same year as the crown prince, was believed to be the brightest, and most erudite and congenial among his classmates. The only fair-haired child in a family of brunettes, he was, the family believed, better looking than even his royal counterpart: *Mashallah,* may God protect him from the evil eye! My brother Javid was exceptionally handsome, but no one dared say that to his face, for he, a fierce debater, would surely find it "a most superficial statement." At only seventeen, he was among the few young men who headed the Jewish Iranian Students Organization. *Mashallah, mashallah!* Two weeks after a phone line, with the easy-to-remember number 891-444, was finally installed in our house, we all came to the conclusion that it was Javid's private line we had just installed. "Invite Hemingway to the Hakakians' for a day," Bez said, "and he would never again wonder for whom the bell tolls." Sometimes Father expressed his irritation by reminding us that a telephone was to be used only in emergencies: "Otherwise why would Alexander Graham Bell bother to call his assistant just to say, 'Watson, come here. I want you,' and hang up? One line is all that should be exchanged on the phone. 'Hi. We are healthy. Good-bye.'"

But even our household of stars had only one genius. Only one shouldered the burden of being the firstborn son, fulfilled everyone's highest expectations, and then went on to impress those tough to please. Only one child's talent had the approval of Queen Farah, her signed letter congratulating him on winning first place in a national drawing contest. Only one of us broke the record for being the youngest cartoonist, at nineteen, on the editorial board of Iran's leading satire magazine, *Tofigh*. With his picture, first from the right in the third row, a thin pubescent mustache making its way through the bushy portraits of editorialists, Albert was the first to put the Hakakian name in boldface print. A thousand *mashallahs!*

Albert's exuberance alone populated our house, his sketches, strewn-about pens, books, brushes, and easels aside. In his spare time, when he was not finishing a commissioned piece or studying to skip a grade, he breathed life into whatever he touched. After he painted our outhouse in art deco style and added a *Mad* magazine rack on the back wall, pissing became the family's favorite outdoor activity. If any of us wanted to take a picture, we asked our subject to say "cheese." Not Albert. He had us name a slew of dairy products until we struck an original pose. To find a new angle, he once made us stand in the corridor that led to the courtyard while he went up to the roof to direct us from the "proper perspective." Mother rushed out of the kitchen screaming, "Come down! You'll fall!" and immediately he knew how he wanted us to pose. His instructions were followed by the buzz of his Polaroid Instamatic in that narrow hallway as, with eight raised arms, eyes cast roofward, four voices chanted, "Come down! You'll fall!" That snapshot captured the memory of one of the last moments when our family was at its most complete, wrapped in Mother's love, always disguised as anxiety, in the small space that was made vast in the bounty of our togetherness.

I understood Albert best by watching him. The callus on the side of his right middle finger, the ink stains on his delicate hands, his tender features—square jaw and straight hair—amounted to a seraphic presence despite his beat-up overalls. Even a grocery list in his handwriting looked like a piece of calligraphy and was hard to throw away. And the photograph on his university ID looked radiant next to the gold royal seal. Name: Albert Hakakian. Place of Birth: Hamedan, Iran. ID Number: 264. Year: Freshman. Campus: The Academy for Visual Arts. Year of Attendance: 1974. That was one year before he left for America, before he flew right out one day and left our family portrait a grin with a missing tooth.

So our fish glided his little body past the angry neighbors, who could not believe their ears. No one, certainly never

an insider, had ever insulted them so by questioning the ways of their idyllic stream. But for everything there is a first, and for that mossy stream, this little fish was indeed a first. And now, swimming breathlessly away from the mob, he was trying to reach the waterfalls and the big, unseen world under it. The little black fish looked down and shuddered. But then he looked behind and saw his friends, who soon would go back to the same old life. What a thought! He took heart and said, "Farewell, my friends. Do not forget me."

✦ ▰◆▰ ✦

"Open your eyes, Roya, or I'll stop reading."

I never took Javid's threats lightly and did as he ordered: "You can't just hear the words. You must also listen very, very carefully."

"Yes. Carefully. Very."

"You can't miss a single thing that happens in a book or in life."

"I promise not to."

But I did. I missed the significance of America that summer when Javid counted one, two, three, and he, Bez, and I lined up in front of Albert and whined, "Khoji, oh, dearest Khoji, for the love of God, please don't go to America!" It was merely banter to me. With that plea, first Javid and then Bez flung himself at Albert. Then it was my turn to top their pile. How we had come to nickname Albert Khoji, I did not care to know, as long as the ring of it turned us into a four-layered sibling cake, my chin digging into Bez's shoulder, my hands at Javid's elbows, my toes rubbing against Albert's thighs. *Don't,* the phrase broke further with each round of repetition, *go,* as the pressure of our weights grew, *please,* and our peals of laughter became brittle cackles, *to,* until each of us panted a syllable of *America*. When Albert, who had squirmed all along, wrested himself out from under the pile, we fell away, and even as we did, we fell upon one another. Our gasps of breath entwined with the hiccups of Father's laughter and Mother's warnings not to crush one another and blanketed us with mirth.

Never in those moments did I realize that something irretrievable was happening. So on a snowy December dawn, as Albert awakened to kiss me good-bye, I, with eyes open to two chinks, protested, "Going is a fine idea, but why must you wake me up to do it?" and without a kiss or another word went back to sleep. Only when Mother called me into the kitchen that night and told me to set the *sofreh*—the cloth we spread on the floor and sat around for meals—with one less plate, one less fork, one less spoon, only faced with this subtraction did I begin to comprehend the sorry mathematics of his departure.

Genius gone! Something in us, in the way we were together, changed thereafter. Letter writing became a family sport. For his sake, we fashioned ourselves into supremely contented individuals on the page. Other than missing him, nothing was ever wrong. Each time, we wrote something cheerful to him, and in doing so, we became a little happier, more magnanimous. His absence made every other defect merely trifling. Mother no longer cooked his favorite meals, but we understood perfectly well that we had to give up enjoying what Albert could not. Out of Father's salary, money had to be set aside to wire to Albert every month. No longer just a family, the Hakakians were a nation guarding the home front while their elite commando fought in faraway lands.

For his part, the commando filed similarly valiant dispatches, needlework letters, sentences painstakingly written on the edges of one of his illustrations, often a map of Iran:

Dearest mother, father, Javid, Behzad, and little (if I may be allowed!) darling Roya:

I kiss your beautiful faces from afar. Except for being away from you, everything is going exquisitely. My English has improved, thanks especially to my job and my studies. Do NOT send me so much money. I really don't need it. But with the last installment, I bought a few surprises that you should receive in the mail soon. . . .

Week after week, the packages came, but since they contained items awe-inspiring but superfluous, we surmised they were pieces of America itself: velvet bow ties, starched, embroidered handkerchiefs, men's denim shorts (sure to signal "queer" in Tehran), black-imprinted T-shirts on whose fronts not our names but those of Albert's favorite sitcom family were inscribed. Now the mailman, too, knew to expect a lunch whenever he had an envelope stamped with the Capitol or the Liberty Bell. We spent days in reverie, imagining the rhythms of life at 500 Riverside Drive in New York City, making friends with a smart Japanese girl named Satomi, stomaching bland American meals, and washing dishes part-time to pay for architecture school. Genius was washing dishes? Why? Why had Albert left the delectable meals at home, especially when he had studied so hard and passed the nationwide university entrance exam and was already a student at the university in Tehran?

In this question, I came face-to-face with the first mystery of my life.

I looked for clues. All that Albert had left behind were some books, a stack of paintings from his first solo exhibit given a few weeks before leaving for America, and several bound volumes of

Tofigh magazine. That year I spent every evening reading *Tofigh* with greater diligence than I did my homework. At first I dreaded an adult publication. But when I discovered that under the pseudonym Roya Hakakian Father had contributed several mildly erotic poems to the magazine, and saw my name in print, pride overcame my apprehension. Besides, everything about *Tofigh* was disarming, and in no time I began to enjoy it: the awkward size of the pages, 11½ by 13½ inches, not exactly the size of a newspaper or magazine; the bright and colorful waxy front and back covers; and most amusing of all, its mascot, Coco, the black human-mouse dressed in tattered poor man's robes, shawls, skullcap, and sandals. With ears perpendicular to the sides of his face and an eggplant for a nose, Coco was as self-deprecating as he was critical. He touted *Tofigh* as the most affordable publication with this weekly reminder:

"Fellow citizen: Do not forget two things on Friday nights: the second, the purchase of a *Tofigh* at a measly 10 rials."

After seeing numerous portraits of the drooling Coco under Sophia Loren's bust or Brigitte Bardot's miniskirt, I finally made a faint connection between those female parts and the nocturnal possibilities of Iran's day off.

Coco spared only the shah and the clergy, but he declared open season on everyone else. His archnemesis was Prime Minister Amir Abbas Hoveida, Coco's target of most biting humor and his avatar of all political wrongs. At least a dozen times in every issue, Hoveida was pictured with his cane, pipe, and wilted orchid pinned to his lapel. Statements Hoveida made, like "Alleviating the needs of the nation is the government's foremost duty," seemed no longer innocuous once they appeared in *Tofigh*. After that one particular statement, the prime minister was illustrated as a jinni barely out of a lamp held in a hoary peasant's hand. The caption under the bowing jinni read: "Except for electricity, water, bread, meat, telephone, transportation, or any other such necessity, I am at your disposal."

Whenever Coco tired of Iranian politics, he needled the rest of the world. After the news broke that following a surgery Elizabeth Taylor could no longer have children, she was depicted on her hospital bed in full makeup, smiling and saying to her doctor, "Thank heavens! For a minute there, I thought you meant I could not have any more husbands." President Johnson was often caricatured, his coat pockets bulging with rockets and grenades, wicks aflame, facing a Vietcong dressed in the same ragged Coco fashion. Next to Moshe Dayan's patched eye, Golda Meir's wrinkles grew deeper with every issue, while Mao Zedong's bust grew larger, spilling over the frames of the pictures as this quote reminded the readers of the virtues of humor on the first page every week: "In the war of life, laughter is the greatest weapon. *Socrates.*"

But in Iran's political war, laughter proved poor ammunition. Tucked between the pages of one of the issues, I found a letter dated June 3, 1974, signed by Hassan Tofigh, editor in chief of the magazine:

Dear Friend, Mr. Albert Hakakian,

With best regards and great gratitude for your collaboration with our publication, we hereby inform you that our magazine has been banned from publication. Our efforts to restore our publication rights have failed, but we are hoping to release a Special Monthly issue, purely, solely, and exclusively a humorous issue, by the end of this month. Please send your material, anything deli-

cious. But beware to supply us with SOLELY humorous material. Tofigh looks forward to an even closer collaboration with you.

Months had passed since the date of that letter, yet the magazine remained shut. Every time I asked an adult why, the mystery became even greater. The reply did not come as words but in a series of gesticulations: Eyes rolled. Teeth bit into lips. Foreheads wrinkled in fear. Hands drew the path of an imaginary knife across throats. Till at last came this whisper: "Shhh! SAVAK!"

That odious acronym! The shah's secret police was the country's most shameful secret. I do not remember when I first learned about it. Like God, SAVAK was ubiquitous and omnipresent in the national imagination. At its mere mention, the psychic clocks were adjusted to 12:01 A.M., the hour when the old civilization of Persia, the glorious "maiden of the Middle East," turned into a destitute girl, fleeing the royal ball in rags.

Dignity was what SAVAK deprived the nation of the most. Beneath its blade, every thinking person split into two: one lived as a private citizen at home; the other lived as a con artist in public, scheming to stay under the agency's radar. To escape its ominous attention, every citizen hid what was on his mind and learned to talk in such a way that his true thoughts would not be obvious. Speaking in metaphors and resorting to poetry were old national traits. But SAVAK gave Iranians yet another reason to aspire to the vague. Conversations did not convey clarity. They became endless games of creating allusions.

It was tough being a child brimming with curiosities among adults who talked in codes. Everyone spoke Persian. Yet the words did not reveal their intentions. They became the hazy outline of the unsaid. I learned to surrender to the strange necessity of obscurity. I learned to accept SAVAK as a mind-bending riddle that could not be solved. I knew to fear it. I knew not to ask about it. I knew it had to do with the shah. And I knew no more. But reading the bound volume of *Tofigh,* learning that it was shut down, somehow led me to suspect a connection between Albert's drawings and his departure. That there was a mystery in that letter and in the pages of the magazine was clear to me. It was also clear that the truth had to be unearthed.

Coiled on a rock under the sun, the little black fish saw a lizard. He called out to the lizard, "Dear lizard, I'm a little black fish who wants to find the end of this stream. You seem wise and worldly, so may I ask you a question?" The lizard nodded: "Of course, ask whatever you like." The little black fish said, "How can I be safe from the pelicans along the way?" And the lizard answered, "If you fall into the pouch of the pelican, the only way out is to cut it open. Here is a dagger. Use it if you ever get trapped."

Javid never liked my silence and peppered every story with questions: "Do you know the author of this book?"

"Samad Behrangi. He has a big, bushy mustache and glasses like Albert's. But he is always bundled up in a fluffy scarf and fez."

"Don't tell me all you know of the great Behrangi is that he wears fluffy things. Roya, ahh!" Mr. Perfection gasped in frustration.

I rushed to my own defense: "Well, it must be cold where he lives."

"Bingo! He came from the northeast of Iran. From Azerbaijan. It's freezing there."

"Came?"

"He's dead."

"Was he old?"

"No."

"Was he sick?"

"Not really."

"Does anyone know why he died? Can we ask someone what happened to him?"

"Absolutely not. You must not mention Behrangi to anyone or take this book out of our home. You hear?"

I nodded vehemently. But agreement alone was not good enough for my brother: "Tell me, why do you like this story?"

"Don't know. I just do."

"That isn't a good answer. When you talk like your upstairs lights are out"—he brought his hand to my temple and snapped once—"I'm tempted to call you Ro, Ro—"

I blocked my ears and watched his mouth move to: "Roghiyeh!"

Of all the things he did or said, this irked me the most. Taking the first syllable of my lovely name, he tagged to the end of it an aged witch's name. My hands still on my ears, I watched him chuckle, and when he stopped, I listened again: "You must always think. If you do nothing else in life, remember what I'm telling you: Think! Think of any book as a riddle. Turn it upside down, inside out. Look at every detail, and ask, Why this? Why that? Only then you'll discover something new. Do you do that? Do you look at things like a smart girl, as the bright Roya that you are, or do you skim everything like a silly girl?"

Think! was the command of our household god. *Look closely!*

And following it, I went back to Albert's boxes and, this time, took out his drawings and covered the floor with them. I had seen all of them at his first solo exhibit, held a few weeks before he left. But the hall was crowded that night, and I was squeezed to the side by adults who piled themselves in front of each painting and remained there. This time I was looking at the images alone, more like a detective than a viewer. Yes! That was what I had to become: a girl detective! I decided that unraveling the mystery of Albert's departure was to be my very first test case.

Since looking at them from afar revealed nothing new, I drew near. I squatted among Albert's artwork. Staring hard, I examined them for the tiniest details. The lines. The straight ones. The curved ones. Their dark, sinuous dance on the page. The shades around the furrows. The short lines of crinkles at the edge of the smiles. The dashes of tension around the knuckles. The semicircles protruding from the necks of young men to mark the Adam's apple. The elliptical spring under a bouncing bust. The wit: the hydrant pissing on a befuddled dog. Ink on paper. Black and white. Simple, spare, energetic. His semicircles were drawn perfectly, as if with a caliper. His curves were fluid, his faces animated in expression.

In one of them, a man at a podium spoke fervently to an empty auditorium, while in the next hall, a voluptuous, half-clad woman with cascading hair belly-danced before a full house. What was my brother suggesting? The next was of two figures, one tall, the other short, walking hand in hand. Above the taller person's head, a small bubble hovered. Above the shorter figure's head, the bubble was large enough to make up for the height difference between the two. I imagined myself as the shorter figure and reveled in this particular drawing. Even children, I surmised Albert was saying, could be as tall as grown-ups, if they think big thoughts. What a joy it was to understand it, especially without anyone's help. With renewed enthusiasm, I moved on.

The next drawing was of a college graduate whose cap had been flipped open to an empty head. His eyes were closed. A glum smile was on his lips. This one puzzled me, and instead of lingering over its meaning, I turned my attention to the next one. It was an oil self-portrait: his face buried behind an exaggerated rendition of his square-framed glasses. Next to his head, on the upper right corner of the canvas, the lines of one of his poems were barely legible:

> Go open the door.
> There might be someone there.
> Go open the door.
> There might be a bird. Or a firefly.
> Go open the door.
> If nothing, there will at least be a breeze.
> Or a current of fresh air.

Going! It was a recurring theme. Everyone on the canvas or in books, including the little black fish, was always *going* somewhere. Where they were going exactly was unclear. If I had a notepad like a real detective, I would have jotted down "going" in red ink with large block letters and underlined it several times. In "going" I had stumbled on an important lead. *Think, Roya, think!*

I leaned into the next image. Suddenly a familiar universe, which I recognized in an instant: a fish, the same fish with the bright red eyes, tiny plump body covered with black scales, who had left home, reasoned its way past the snobbish frog, the kindly lizard, the school of benighted seahorses, the clumsy stork, and the evil pelicans, to arrive at the green sea. But it was lynched, hanging lifeless in the middle of the page.

Something dreadful had happened to the little black fish. The picture before me was its evidence. A writer was dead. A magazine had been shut down. As I leafed through the pages of the guest-book and glanced at the signatures of those who had visited the exhibit, I saw notes of admiration but also of apprehension: "So much talent at such a young age is a double-edged sword, Sincerely." "Wish you could see more of the positive in life, Best Regards." "Seeing your show for the second time now. Love your stuff, but be careful!"

Be careful! I remembered hearing those words from Mother's brother Ardi on the opening night. At the end of the evening, he went up to Albert, patted him on the back, and said, "Way to go, Chegi! Way to go!" Father had cringed. In an unusual burst of fury, he told Uncle Ardi not to call Albert by that name.

"Who's Chegi?" I asked Bez.

"Some rebel guy named Che Guevara on the run from the police of his country."

This time Father snapped at Bez and we stopped talking.

The mystery lurked in the "Be carefuls," in Father's sudden flare of anger. He had been the one to turn us all on to reading. He was the one who bought our first subscription to *Tofigh*. He was the chief dervish, the one to thrive on his reputation of being a "spiritual man." To him, anything we could not afford was not worth having. And nothing was more worth having than books. But he had never expected his idea of culture, what he called "washing one's hands from all material things," to lead to armed rebels wandering in the mountains of Latin America.

That night, Uncle Ardi followed his apology to Father with a suggestion: "It wouldn't be bad to send him away, Hakakian. Send him to America, till his head cools off! Far away from——" Shhh!

Albert's departure had to do with his paintings. My brother's art, the essence of his genius, had separated him from our family. That much I knew. And I wanted Albert to know I was aware and no longer the sleepy, oblivious child who had let him down by letting him go without even a kiss. I wanted him to know that while he was at 500 Riverside Drive bettering himself, his sister at number three Alley of the Distinguished was doing the same. And that I had grown old enough to learn his secret and keep it.

So I forged my own potion of allusions and began a letter to him:

Dear Khoji, no no sorry, dear Mr. Albert,

I would like to take this opportunity to write you a letter. I am proud of you. I hope you like your new friends. What funny names they have: Bill, Jack, Joe. One syllable each! Father says, you can cough and make a sound better than that. Haha! I hope I made you laugh. I read a lot now. Iran is our country. Our flag has three colors: green, white and red. Green is its uppermost color. Streams are too small. Little fishes love the sea. Sometimes so much they must disobey their mothers and swim to the sea. Our flag waves proudly in the wind. Iran is our beloved motherland. Bye.

3

THE BABY BLUE BMW

EVERY YEAR, THREE WEEKS BEFORE PASSOVER, WE, THE Hakakians, assumed our annual pose of piety. To honor the ancient Israelites' hasty departure from Egypt, we hastened ourselves, rallying around Mother, to wage our own crusade. Our enemies were not at all alike: the slaves had fought against Pharaoh, whereas we fought against dirt. Yet a feeling of urgency descended upon number three Alley of the Distinguished. And so we armed ourselves with an arsenal of brooms, rags, mops, scrubs, and sprays.

We awoke at dawn, when the "cotton beater" made his yearly visit. He camped in the corner of the courtyard, stripped our quilts and mattresses, and removed all the cotton inside. Then squatting among the heap, he brought out a harplike tool. Holding it amid the heap, he plucked at its coarse strings till the flattened cotton, caught in the strings, separated and regained their fluffiness. The muffled notes of his tool and the white cloud that surrounded him were all that we heard or saw of him till dusk.

Inside the house, we got busy. We brought down the curtains, dusted every rod, rolled every rug, and swept underneath everything. After searching our closets, we emptied our wallets and handbags, unrolled our pant cuffs, lined up every jacket and pair of trousers on the clothesline, and turned the pockets inside out. We stretched the corner of a rag over our index finger, traced along the sides of each drawer to the four corners, and twirled our fingertip around a few times. The merriment would come only when seriousness had been paid its due.

For those three weeks, we attached biblical meaning to every tiny deviation from the routine of our household. In the holiday microcosm that formed in our kitchen, we saw signs of the divine: The Red Sea at the foot of our thawing refrigerator, as golden shafts of light, emanating from its open door, parted the gloomy fluorescence of the kitchen. The gas burner, which we wheeled out of the storage, was our occasional burning bush. In a vat over it, we boiled water and dipped perfectly clean dishes to scald away any trace of the non–"kosher for Passover" foods. And our savior, our seasonal Moses, our year-round Job, Mother, with an outstretched arm, lamenting her migraine, led us in battle against dirt.

I never questioned why we cleaned with far greater zeal than we celebrated the freedom of the Jews. But since our life teemed with metaphors, the cleaning frenzy, too, had a meaning greater than met the eye. Passover was our only opportunity to flaunt our faith before the public. It was a time for our neighbors to see into our gutted life, to witness our diligence in cleaning, for however far Iran had come, even by 1977, some Muslims still called Jews *najes:* dirty. This was the season to prove our cleanliness to our neighbors, though as I would soon learn, the war against impurity was without end, and uncleanness a most indefatigable enemy.

Just as the cleaning fury was inevitable every year, so was the seder at my maternal grandmother's home. Seated around the Passover *sofreh,* everyone chattered for as long as Father let them. Mother, Aunt Zarrin, and Grandmother briefed one another on the details of the preparation ordeals, every year more complicated than the one before. There was always a crisis requiring an eleventh-hour intervention: "Avram, the winemaker, had a stroke." Tsk, tsk! Could there ever be a Passover without wine? "But A.J., God keep him safe and sound for a hundred and twenty years, made our own wine at home." Aunt Zarrin cast a boastful look her husband's way, while Mother repeated the story to Father. (Nothing like stirring a bit of rivalry between the husbands of the two sisters!) Cousin Farah kept at her favorite task, cracking a hard-boiled egg against her plate and shelling it, for an egg would soon be needed to make a blessing. The last tale was topped. Grandmother had nearly fallen off the ladder—*Oh, Mother, why do you never pick up the phone and say you need help?*— trying single-handedly to wipe the spiderwebs off the ceiling corners. Farah cracked another egg, while through the fading tsks, Mother entered the contest: "And I slaved over the stove for a week making almond brittle"—Bez and I cringed at the mention—"and two children, I won't name names, overdosed on every last bit."

But the smell of saffron coming from the kitchen, and the feast before us, were proof that those troubles merited no more attention. The complaints ebbed. Their voices merged into a joint sigh, a yearning really, expressed in a question: "How will Albert celebrate this night?"

My uncles huddled around Father, briefing him on their own news, the latest in the car and life insurance business. But a "This, too, shall pass!" was all they could expect from him. On the eve of Passover, he refused to hear of any woes but those of his ancestors toiling away in Egypt. "Majid dear, are we ready to start? Is everything in place?" he would say to Mother's fourth and sweetest brother, the delighted deputy, who bellowed, "Right away, Hakakian!" Hakakian! That was how they addressed Father. Neither by "Mr." nor by his first name. Only by his last name, a perfect sign of their fond regard. They were younger than Father by at least a decade. They had all been students in his school, and around him they remained children, forever trying their best to behave.

After tallying the seder items, Uncle Majid announced, "All's good to go!" And just as Father tapped his spoon against a glass to begin, someone, usually Aunt Zarrin, pleaded, "For the love of God, Hakakian, wait five more minutes!"

The extra five minutes passed, but the person who was keeping us all did not arrive. Father began. At first he only hummed to himself, but gradually he made an audible blessing over what he was tasting, and when he had summoned a few amens, he rose to his feet, the Haggadah in his right hand, the cup of wine in his left, and recited the opening prayers. The family pretended to be listening. But what everyone was really listening for was the sound of a baby blue BMW and its driver, Uncle Ardi. The seder was incomplete without him, though no one was alarmed by his lateness. Why be alarmed when we knew that what was keeping Uncle Ardi could only be an exquisite meal, an irresistible woman, or a major insurance deal?

But that year, an hour into the ceremony, Father was the only one still reading on. Grandmother, Aunt Zarrin, and Mother whispered their hopes and worries to one another: "He's on his way for sure." "He'd never miss a seder." "Could he have car trouble?" Those who heard that last question shook their heads: Uncle Ardi would sooner lose an arm than allow any trouble to befall his car. My uncles frowned and pondered: the snags at the office, the clients to tend to. Uncle Majid leafed through his phone book to see whom he should call. And then, through the windows of Grandmother's living room, came the sound of a key turning, two latches lifting, four iron hinges squeaking, and the rumblings of relief, *vroom! vroom!*, a car engine going off, ending the anxieties.

Everyone looked to the hallway door to catch the first glimpse of the beloved phantom. Uncle Ardi, hoping to enter unnoticed, snuck inside. Walking toward us, he had already begun muttering a blessing, any random blessing he could think of, and fussing with the yarmulke that, lodged amid his dark, curly hair, never needed adjusting. So relieved were the guests that their words of grievance sounded no worse than a greeting. Only my uncles gave him an unforgiving look from the corner of their eyes, with the promise of a serious talk yet to come. "Amen! Amen!" repeated Uncle Ardi, dismissing everyone and making his way over to Father, still at his task. He knelt and kissed Father on the forehead: "May you live long, Hakakian! Your breath is the breath of Eden." Father raised his head, rested his glasses on his forehead, beamed a grin, and shook his head in disapproval: "Ardi! Ardi! Ardi!"

Ardi indeed! Being the family's dream, I saw Uncle Ardi as our most glorious reality. He appeared and with him came the whispers of the admiring crowd: "There's a solid man for you. Only twenty-seven, but a solid, solid man!" He strutted around a room, greeting everyone, embracing some, shaking the hands of others, freshening their drinks. His elegant posture restored dignity to the tackiest of haberdashery. In his eyes was a volcano that, when active, drew the female kind to the path of its hazel lava. "Such a solid, solid man right there for you!" Little seemed to matter to anyone who stole his glance, for once cast, it shone with the wish to behold nothing else, as he asked: "On my dear life, is there anything I can possibly get you?" The solid, solid man, leaning gently into the other, purred in a tone of perfect surrender.

Everyone in the family had daily dealings with non-Jews and made friends with a few along the way. But Uncle Ardi barely mingled with the Jewish community. In his retinue there was always an Ali, a Hassan, or a Mohammad, names distinctly, and to the family, jarringly, Muslim. The envious in the family thought of his popularity as pathology and diagnosed him with "friendosis." But reveling in it, Uncle Ardi cherished his friends, and called himself a hale "friendophile" and boasted, "If I have twenty friends, nineteen of them are Muslims."

Nineteen—what a number! Only one less than twenty, the Iranian equivalent of a hundred, the grade of all grades in school. The single touch of red ink on an otherwise pristine black-and-white exam sheet. The charm of the slight imperfection. A step below perfection, below estrangement. The Jew on the verge of slipping away. The Jew whose accent adopted the inflections of the Jewish dialect only when he chose to. Where the Persian syllable required a rise, Jews dipped their stress; where it required a dip, they dipped their stress even more: their intonation sank, just the way they hid their heads in their collars in small, anti-Semitic towns.

But not Uncle Ardi's stresses. He was the Jew who had shed the "ghetto" speech, Persian peppered with Hebrew. Even Jews mistook him for a Muslim and behaved as they did in the company of one. They offered him the best seat in the house and waited cheerfully on him. They watched their manners and spoke flawless Persian, even quoted passages from the holy Koran: "What a wonderful prophet you have, Mr. Ardi. How full of wisdom is his book. I read it often. Last night I came across this: Chapter Cow, verse 122, I quote, 'Hear me, O Jews: thou art the chosen people.'"

"You take me for a goy, don't you?" Uncle Ardi would say, reverting to the insider dialect.

And the amiable host, regaining friskiness, protesting Uncle Ardi's indiscernible ways, would begin anew: "You know, Mr. Ardi, this Muhammad they call a prophet, may his head catch on fire, was illiterate. He paid a learned Jew to ghostwrite the Koran. And when the Jew finished writing, he inscribed 'A, L, M' on the top page. Just three letters. And the goyim think it's a code. You want me to break it? *Ayn lo mamashot.* Meaning 'Nothing's true here!' What prophet? He was a warmonger, I tell you. An illiterate warmongering bandit is all he was!"

When Uncle Ardi lingered long enough to have tea, he also got an earful about the Jews—the bounced checks, the broken promises, and how unreliable or duplicitous they could be—stories that always ended in: "I'd not swap one rotten strand on a goy's head with a hundred on a Jew's."

To all this Uncle Ardi listened, and in reply, he admired the tea.

He did not think ghetto thoughts. He had made a safe passage to the other side, even shed the ghetto jobs: he wasn't a butcher or a salesman, a teacher or gold trader, but an insurance man. He was so assimilated, so certain of his prospects in Iran, that he even insured Muslims. And his rates were some of the most reasonable around: liability for any four-cylinder vehicle only 500 tomans a year, roughly $80. Six cylinders: 850 tomans! Guaranteed by Asia Insurance Co., a division of the world-trusted Lloyds of London.

What Uncle Ardi had really shed was fear, the fear of claiming his share of the good life like any other middle-class citizen. But he did not call it fear. Instead he said, "I know how to live." And the place where he knew best to live, where he belonged, was Iran. Everything about him was Iranian, even his name: Ardi, short for Ardeshir, the king of an ancient Persian empire. He was so settled that he was even willing to invest in vanity, to buy depreciating goods—like a BMW. No other car would have matched his optimism, the exuberant claim he laid to Tehran. Tehran and no other city. And never more confidently than in 1977.

Naturally, it caused an uproar at the seder when Father asked Uncle Ardi to read the Ha Lachma. Everyone burst into laughter, even before he began. He obeyed and read, but not without a touch of subversion, a bit of mischief:

"'This is the bread of affliction'—some affliction!—'that our forefathers ate in the land of Egypt. This year we are slaves.' May this slavery never end! 'This year here and next year at home in Israel.' Pardon me for not packing!"

Tissues passed hands as the guests wiped their eyes and roared with laughter. Without missing a beat, Father corrected Uncle Ardi's every word. He was the unruly child Father loved enough to punish. One man resisted. The other pressed. Neither relented. So many tears of joy were shed that night. It was as if everyone knew the tears they were to shed in the coming weeks would all be of sadness.

The family was laughing not at Uncle Ardi and Father but with them. The words recited at the seder conjured no immediate bitter memory in the minds of anyone except the few elders. "Bondage," "affliction," and "suffering at the hands of a bad majority" meant little to most of them. They vowed, "Next year in Israel," but knew, even as the words rang in the air, how hollow they were. The family dreamed of the land of milk and honey but wanted to wake up in Tehran. Business was booming, and my uncles, the entrepreneurs, did not want to be fettered by a history that seemed distant now. For nearly half a century, the 100,000 Jews of Iran had been sending a representative of their choice to the Majles. They were at last living in any neighborhood they chose to, and the only remaining ghetto was in the far south of the city, where the poor of every race or creed lived. Even *najes* was seldom heard in public. Iran was at its most welcoming to Jews in all of its history.

Why even speak of leaving when Tehran's allure was greater than ever? The median income had doubled over the past decade. On the etiquette chart, generosity and lavish spending had soared to number one. Uncle Ardi vied for the check at restaurants, and though he was not the only one trying to grab it, he was often the one to reach into his wallet and quietly pay it. Nightlife was flourishing, and between tending to clients and romancing women, he was also the official family gourmand and walking *Zagat*. The hosts of the upper Pahlavi Avenue restaurants wasted no time in clearing their best table for him. At Chattanooga, only those accompanying Uncle Ardi were handed menus, because "Beef Stroganoff, easy on the cream, followed by the chocolate soufflé" was the order the waiter did not need to be told. When he did not feel like driving, he walked to the shops across from the University of Tehran. At Arezoumanian's, "the family that unlocked the secret to a good sandwich," his favorite mortadella sandwich was served on a round tray beside a shot of chilled vodka. And before he headed for the office, he stopped not for the traditional tea, yogurt, or sour cherry drink but for a cup of café au lait or something befitting his own bubbly nature, usually a bottle of Pepsi. By nightfall, long after the secretary had gone home, the tune of the two telephones on his desk changed from the daytime duet to the solo serenades on his private line. Even late into the evening, Uncle Ardi did not stop selling insurance. But what he insured after hours was happiness: a commodity he peddled exclusively at one of several cabarets, but on Thursday nights only at Moulin Rouge.

If the family was laughing, this year a little harder than ever, it was also because everyone secretly delighted in what had kept Uncle Ardi later than ever; in *who* had kept Uncle Ardi later than ever. Once upon a time, there was a woman named Neela who received one of Uncle Ardi's molten glances but, in return, cast a look of her own, an eruption more spectacular than his, which made Uncle Ardi melt, before his family's astonished eyes, into a man-droplet. And their story had just begun.

This particular seismological incident had occurred several weeks earlier, during a family picnic in Darband, the camping grounds of north Tehran. Our group arrived in a half dozen cars, the extended family along with friends and colleagues of my uncles. It was the thirteenth and last day of the Iranian New Year celebration. To keep away the evil omen of thirteen from their homes, families spent the day outdoors. Jews also participated in the festivity, since it marked the arrival of spring and was a secular tradition.

When Father finally stopped the car, I darted out. Darband's unrivaled landscape propelled me to do so. In Darband, only cars and people were at eye level. Everything else lay on two distant planes, far beneath and high above, each stunning in its own way. The ravine below looked like a green trampoline standing on pillars of poplar and walnut trees. What kept me from springing onto it, if not good sense, was the sound of reality: the roaring rapids of the river, invisible from where I stood, that snaked through the trees. And above, the grand Alborz mountain range filled me with the wish to fly. I knew if I asked permission to go hiking, I would be told it was not for girls to climb mountains. So, I gazed at those heights, at the snow-capped peak, Damavand, and secretly vowed to climb my way to its summit someday.

We descended the steep steps through the rocky bed of Darband into the heart of the ravine, carrying our pillows and bags. At the bottom, each family settled on a wooden bed by the river, spread a kilim over it, and piled their pillows on one side. Others built a nest of stone at the river's edge where their cantaloupes and watermelons cooled. Women lit the braziers, while men slipped into their pajama pants and plopped themselves down around the backgammon sets. I kept one eye on the biography of Marie Curie I was reading and another on the fantastic troubles of the adults, who, overpowered by the sound of the river and the birds, had to scream to be heard. With each skitter of dice, I saw Father's lips move, and my mind filled the gaps of his inaudible bravura: "By the time I'm done with you, you'll be so dead, the birds in these trees will be singing your eulogy."

And his opponent, Uncle A.J., fired back, "Stick to teaching, Hakakian, because your game stinks!"

But when Grandmother craned her neck and elbowed Aunt Zarrin, who elbowed Mother, who elbowed Cousin Farah, I put down the book and moved nearer to them. Because I was too young to be elbowed, I fashioned a personal reconnaissance I thought of as human osmosis: learning the untold by breathing in its vicinity. Years later, I realized that the proper term for the technique was journalism.

Uncle A.J.'s Muslim colleague, Mr. Maroof, was just stepping off the stairs, and for the first time, he had brought his wife and two daughters along on an outing with our family. Initially all eyes were on Mrs. Maroof, the wife of a seemingly modern man, wrapped in such outdated garb as a black veil. Very few women appeared veiled in the northern parts of Tehran. The ones who did were mostly maids, and they wore not black but floral-patterned veils, held loosely by the arms about them. Instead of religiosity, the floral-patterned veil signaled class, mostly lower-middle, and bad style, since it usually covered an unkempt appearance.

However, as Mrs. Maroof's daughters came into view, our gaze shifted to them, to their blouses and miniskirts, especially to the older beauty, Neela. Running after her, Uncle A.J. rushed to introduce her to the family and shouted, "Neela, let me tell you who you need to know here and who you need to stay away from."

She stopped, put down her bags, and turned to look at him. But instead of Uncle A.J., it was Uncle Ardi who was standing in front of her. Uncle A.J. probably introduced him as the one Neela should stay away from. But from where I stood, it seemed clear she was looking at the only one she needed to know.

It was at this moment that I moved closer to Grandmother. Somewhat vexed, she quietly groaned to Aunt Zarrin, "Look how she is eating him up with her eyes." The men ogled Neela and would have continued to if Uncle A.J. had not proposed that we play a game of charades. Everyone welcomed the idea, and the air of awkwardness lifted in the bustle of preparation for the game. The wooden benches were rearranged into two rows. Each team settled in one row. All of us, old, young, veiled, and unveiled, were now teammates. The Maroofs and the rest of us blended together. Winning was on everyone's mind.

Yet something changed in the presence of the Maroofs. Something always changed when a Muslim showed up among us. It was not a change I could describe by adjectives: good, bad, happy, or sad. It was a tiny shift, almost physical, from languor to alertness. Being with the family and among Jews was effortless, like being in my pajamas. Being among Muslims, friends or neighbors, was like being in my party dress. I was careful not to stain or wrinkle it. The fabric itched. The zipper pinched. I had to adjust myself to fitting into something less familiar. But it also gave me the chance to see myself anew. It took effort being in it, but I liked the way it changed me. I liked how I looked in it. I liked how all of us reshuffled to put on our dress as a family, to make room for the Maroofs.

Once everyone was engrossed in the game, Uncle Ardi stealthily walked over and wedged himself between Farah and me, said a few words in her ear, wrote his office phone number on the flap of a matchbook, and gave it to her discreetly. Minutes later, she was sitting next to Neela, who lit her father's cigarette with the matchbook in her hand.

If the family was in more of an uproar at this seder than ever, it was also at the surprise of the unexpected, the tantalizing twist in the predictable plots of Uncle Ardi's amorous stories. For the first time, our invincible hero showed tremors of vulnerability. The elders thought of Uncle Ardi's affairs with non-Jewish women as mild afflictions—some lingered longer than others but all eventually passed. The rest of the family also presumed he would move on, yet reveled in seeing how it would happen.

After reciting the Ha Lachma, Uncle Ardi asked, "So, Hakakian, are your bags packed or is the flight to Jerusalem postponed for another year?"

Father smiled and waved him away, assuming his question had been meant in jest. But Uncle Ardi, without the slightest hint at humor, pressed on: "Really, Hakakian, why say it? Why not leave it at 'Love thy neighbor like thyself!' and call off the rest?"

Only after Father removed his glasses and I saw the lines of a certain disquiet form on his forehead did I sense Uncle Ardi's seriousness. The uncle whose presence always comforted everyone suddenly looked uneasy. His lips paled. His cheeks twitched. He averted his gaze from Father's. All the laughter had stopped. Silence dominated the room. Father cleared his throat, readying himself for an answer. But sensing the potential for an untimely argument, Grandmother called everyone to dinner. Father waved again and said, "Later, later!" And Uncle Ardi excused himself and left the room.

That night, the holiday feast was more exquisite than ever. The Chinese apples had been in season. So Aunt Zarrin's Chinese apple-and-plum beef stew had a luscious, tangy sweetness. The stew gave off a coppery steam and was served in white china bowls with etchings of a droopy-eyed Omar Khayyam around the edges. Grandmother had dusted off the family's old recipe for tarragon veal ball. Tarragon was exceptionally popular that year, since the darling herbalist of the nation's housewives, Doctor Jazayeri, raved about its virtues, week after week, on his radio show. Though she shared that recipe with everyone, no one quite mastered the magical texture only she could create: at the first touch of a fork, every round, solid ball opened like a gift to reveal a sweet surprise at the core, a date, a prune, or a few raisins, a mystery every time. Mother had outdone herself, too. The cumin scent of her stuffed chicken with jasmine rice and yellow split peas had suffused the air and strengthened the appetites all through the seder. The trays of rice topped with mounds of currants and almond shreds drew the most attention, because the guests knew what was to come next. First came the sounds of the skimmer banging against the bottom of the pot. And soon the plates of rice crusts, nearly fried, gilded with saffron, passed hands and were finally placed at the center of the *sofreh,* amid the plates of mint, basil, and radishes.

Later that week, drifting in and out of sleep on Farah's bed, I heard her whisper into the phone that Neela and Uncle Ardi's relationship was turning into a smashing romance. Some weeks later, I found snapshots hidden under the same bed, pictures of the couple weathering their first seasons of intimacy: Uncle Ardi's arms around Neela, the two of them standing under the budding plane trees on Elizabeth Boulevard; Uncle Ardi and Neela by the Caspian Sea, their weekend getaway spot. There she was in a one-piece swimsuit in his arms, splayed like an offering he had brought to bestow upon the god of camera. In another picture, Neela sat on the hood of the BMW while Uncle Ardi, one foot on the tire, reached to kiss her. Only one photo included other people and that had been taken indoors, in the family's seaside cottage. In it, everyone beamed with joy. Mr. Maroof had one hand on Uncle Ardi's back and rested the other affectionately on his chest, like he was receiving him, claiming him as his own. And Mrs. Maroof lifted her daughter's hand to show it off to the camera: there was a diamond ring on Neela's finger.

A discovery of Agatha Christie proportions! I had gained this new knowledge by means far more sophisticated than mere osmosis. All on my own, I had pieced together two of the family's greatest secrets: first, the reason for Albert's departure, and now, the engagement of Uncle Ardi. This was a piece of gossip worth a tidal wave of elbowing. But even though I was very excited, I knew I could not tell anyone about it. I, too, was smitten with the couple's grace and the tangible bliss in the pictures and felt compelled to keep quiet. This poignant moment, the sudden exercise of restraint, was an electrifying transformation. And I recognized it as my passage into a glorious new age, into puberty, though the actual physical changes that occurred a year later proved to be terribly anticlimactic.

"Why her?" Farah kept asking her confidantes on the telephone. Her beauty? But every man, she reasoned, was bound to get irritated by a woman his own height, tire of her fashionable slenderness, and yearn for womanly plumpness. It would be a matter of days before he saw her nose not as exotic but as deformedly hooked. Was it her hair? Eh, no intelligent man would ever bank on something as fickle as hair. Her upbringing and family? Uncle Ardi, so urbane, could not possibly want to associate himself with a mother-in-law so devoutly clad. But that convinced neither Farah nor the listener on the other end. Mrs. Maroof's veil was the remnant of an extinct era. A relic from the 1930s: before Reza Shah ordered the mandatory unveiling of all women and sent gendarmes to the streets to pull the veils off women's heads. Her veil was not a symbol of her faith but of the human reluctance to rid oneself of something old and familiar. Mrs. Maroof had been thrilled by the great reforms of 1962—"women granted the right to vote!"—and of 1967—"women granted the right to divorce!" She celebrated the promises that Iran's new future held for her daughters; thus her embrace of an unprecedented fashion: the hot pants and the bikinis on Neela and her sister.

It was Neela's spirit, then, that had captivated Uncle Ardi, Farah concluded, after she had reasoned her way out of every other possibility. She paused over the telephone. Yes, the answer was Neela's spirit, a spirit not only hers but theirs. A spirit she and Uncle Ardi shared, one of optimism. At only twenty-three, Neela earned a good living modeling and selling jewelry and Uncle Ardi was already a partner in the Asia Insurance Company. Unlike the disenchanted mascot of *Tofigh,* Coco, they were pleased with the status quo. And since neither had attended university, they read little, knew even less about the little black fishes and the fates of their writers or the constraints of . . . *shhh!*

They also shared the outlook of a new generation, one that had cast off religion and tradition. Why else would they drive a BMW instead of an Iranian-manufactured Paykan? They accepted no homegrown hero, followed the lead of no guru who was not blond. If they were going to learn about the power of love, it was not from Rumi but from Roger Moore. If they were going to emulate anyone, in chivalry, for instance, it would not be Imam Ali but John Wayne. If they were to climb anything, it would not be Mount Sinai but the Empire State Building: a mighty couple, with the world's possibilities at their mighty feet.

At last Grandmother, Aunt Zarrin, and Mother came together to fight Neela. The battle began morbidly, as most events began in Iran: The women, dressed in black, started to make daily visits to Grandfather's grave site. On Saturdays, the men gathered in Grandmother's living room to say prayers of remorse and for-giveness. They arrived unshaved, sat on the chairs, rocked to and fro, recounted the penance the prophets had paid, as if recount-ing their own, over and over, and stopped only to sip tea, to wet their parched throats, so they could read on.

The kitchen was just as crowded. Herbalists left on the heels of astrologers. The astrologers exited when the palm readers entered. On the stove, miniature pots appeared. Something was always bubbling, steaming. Someone was always stirring, reading a spell. Stirring again, saying the same spell with eyes closed. Stir-ring some more, repeating the words again, then adding a pinch of this, a dash of that, but never tasting. The ultimate potion, often a dark, viscous liquid, was added to Uncle Ardi's meals. At the kitchen window, Grandmother, leaning out, pleaded with someone: "Do something, I beg you!" I first thought she was speaking to a neighbor but realized later that she was pleading with my dead grandfather not to lose an opportunity to involve God: "May light shower your grave, Isaac! You're the nearest to Him."

Until Uncle Ardi's affair, being a Jew had been a blithe experience for me. It was a license, unearned, to receive special privileges: an extra day off from school on Saturdays, an additional new year in every year, endless holidays every season. It was a pass to exceptional places: to the stage as a dancer at the Royal Court of King Xerxes and Queen Esther; in Father's arms to cross a wide canal on our way to the synagogue; in a pool of light at the threshold of the synagogue under elaborate chandeliers; within the range of the rosewater flask of the temple's keeper, who welcomed each congregant with a dash; before a grieving mourner who offered a slice of onion quiche for a blessing; between the men's and the women's aisles, crisscrossing to deliver messages of wives to husbands, secret lovers, and their rivals; at the foot of the altar, watching a boy rise, recite a few prayers, and step down a man. Being a Jew was to expect a surprise from the ordinary: like two wooden panels that, once unlocked, revealed a treasure of scrolls draped in layers of crimson velvet and gold-embroidered white lace, melodious with bells atop each; or a single glass that, shattering under a young man's foot, broke the hush of hundreds in a wedding ballroom. Being a Jew was to be a humble number in God's math: adult men, saying kaddish, hid their faces under their prayer shawls and wept like children.

But seeing the family react to Uncle Ardi's affair with Neela, I felt the blitheness waning. I became leery of God, whose love had once come so easily to me. I became wary of my family, its lugubrious underlife, its lugubrious wrath, and the lugubrious practices that had come so easily to them. I examined and reexamined every encounter with the Maroofs. I pondered our day in Darband. The verdant spaces where we had come together with them yellowed in my memory. Had they truly been green? The sounds of nature, the birds, the rapids, the rustle of the poplar leaves—were they there to envelop us equally, bind us equally? The wooden benches. They creaked. The Maroofs sat next to Father, Mother, Aunt Zarrin, and Uncle A.J. and played charades. Mr. Maroof pretended to be a baker. Uncle Ardi, his assistant, rolled a make-believe pin over the dough and slapped it against the walls of a make-believe oven. Each performed so well that Grandmother guessed their job in seconds. Was that the real game of charades, or was it the whole of our afternoon, the attempt at shedding our differences to become one? Oh, how we had scrubbed, boiled, combed, brushed, and bleached. We were no less clean, see? Or were we trying to say that we were cleaner?

On a Saturday afternoon, Grandmother's hallway door swung violently open and Uncle Ardi stormed into the kitchen. "Do you think I don't know what you've been up to?" he shouted at Grandmother. He pushed the hair away from his forehead and pointed to it: "Do you see 'idiot' written across here?"

She lowered herself into a chair, repeating, "What in God's name, Ardi?"

Aunt Zarrin rested her arm around Grandmother's shoulder. Mother pleaded with Uncle Ardi to take a seat. He would not. She fetched him a glass of water. It stayed on the table. The kitchen was too small for all of them and the secret that had brewed in it for weeks. The words had to be spoken. The name had to be said. Uncle Ardi said it: "I'm going to marry Neela. This week. And if you try to stop me, I'll just take her hand and go." Without a destination, his threat did not have gravity. So he added, "To Qom."

Qom, as in the Vatican of Iran! No one went to Qom but pilgrims to visit the holy Muslim shrines. No one lived there but clerics. There was nothing to do there but study at a seminary. But Uncle Ardi had other business: "I'll have a mullah marry us in Qom." This was his way of saying he would convert if they got in his way.

Aunt Zarrin wobbled a few steps till she steadied herself against the refrigerator. Mother pressed the back of her hand against her forehead. Grandmother rose to her feet. She walked slowly to the utensil drawer. The drawer rattled open. In a world of her own, Grandmother was mumbling to herself, as she did sometimes, looking for a spice container or a missing key. A few more clattering sounds punctuated the silence in the kitchen. "Aha!" she finally exclaimed. The search had ended.

Her best butcher knife in one hand, she turned to face everyone. Gripping the knife's black handle, her fingers appeared whiter than usual. She pressed the point of the knife against her chest, and no longer mumbling, she said, "I'll put this through my heart if you . . ."

The sentence lingered in the air, incomplete. Mother rushed to grab the knife from her. Uncle Ardi stormed out of the kitchen. Aunt Zarrin rushed after him. She called his name. No answer came but doors banging. Then came the sound of an engine. Aunt Zarrin had caught up with Uncle Ardi in the court-yard. Talking through the driver's-side window, she was pleading with him. But we could not hear her words. The car started. Aunt Zarrin kept on talking through the furious roars of the engine. He backed out. She ran alongside the car, still talking. But he sped away. Aunt Zarrin stood at the door, still. She walked to the mid-dle of the block and looked to each end. She walked back and slapped the back of her hand. She was fuming but weakening, too. Hunched, her knees half-bent, she stood in the middle of the courtyard. Feeble and disbelieving, she limped back to the street and looked to either side again. Then she shut the door. The hinges clicked into place and she evanesced into the corridor. Only her voice reverberated against the walls: "He'll ruin us. We'll be shamed. He'll speed and kill himself. Or he'll marry Neela. A goy! And make my Farah a spinster for good."

Two days passed before news of Uncle Ardi came. A call came from the sheriff of a small town near the family cabin by the Caspian Sea. Uncle Ardi was in custody. In his mad drive, he had run over an elderly man who was now in the intensive care unit. Uncle Majid instantly posted bail and a court date was set. But would there be justice, especially if the old man died? A Jew had run over a Mus-lim, in a small northern town. The incident was likely to transcend the bounds of a traffic case and become a matter of honor for the people of that town. Even as popular and as loved as Uncle Ardi was, he feared standing trial in so remote a place.

Within forty-eight hours, Uncle Ardi was packed for that

unimaginable destination, Israel. There was no time for proper good-byes with his fans, friends, colleagues, or even with Neela. He went without fanfare, leaving the family to itself, to its yearning for him. Grandmother's courtyard became a monument to his absence: The BMW sat without a driver. It was all the solidity that was left of that solid, solid man. The family resumed its life again, now that Neela was no longer a threat. More than anyone else, Aunt Zarrin credited herself for the break between the couple. She believed that her last plea with Uncle Ardi in the courtyard, just before he drove away, had made all the difference. Through the driver's-side window, she had begged him before he took off, "Don't do it. Not because of me, Mother, or anyone else. Not even because you'd make Father's soul uneasy in his grave for all eternity. Don't do it for Farah. No decent Jew would ever marry a girl whose uncle has married a Muslim."

4

FARAH

THE LAST TIME FARAH STOOD BEFORE HER VANITY MIRROR as a single girl, I was in the room. On a day in May 1978, Farah, who had just turned nineteen, was getting ready for her future in-laws' formal visit. To be in Farah's presence when she prettied herself was to be a privileged insider, witnessing the operations of a lone goddess. Nowhere else was she in such formidable command. She greeted the mirror as if a higher power inhabited it. She turned and tilted her head, each time a little higher, a little lower, slightly to the left or right, smiling with her mouth closed or open for a few teeth to show. If there were any gods in her mirror, they gave her confidence by assuring her that a beauty so abundant as hers deserved abundant happiness. Then she went to work, starting with her hair. She pondered the sizes of her brushes before she chose one. At her mirror, nothing befuddled Farah, not even the dizzying range of powders, blushes, and lipsticks. Shadows were her only weakness, as she sometimes had trouble applying them without having them dust her eyelashes.

That night, she exhausted her repertoire. Throwing a damp towel over the rollers, she ironed her hair for a frizz-free do. Then she handed me a jar of cream and asked that I cover the freckles on her back: "In small, gentle circular motions, like so," she said, drawing with her index finger in the air. She sprayed even the folds behind her knees with perfume, making me wonder just what could possibly bring a nose to that vicinity. Several times I was about to scream, especially when she held the iron against her hair, or squeezed the blackheads she alleged were on her forehead till her skin broke, or tweezed the crescents of her eyebrows into barely visible wisps. Every time I protested, she paused, threw her head back, and with imperial certainty told me that beauty never came without pain. Pause. She spoke slowly because she believed slowness was the indisputable mark of adulthood. Then she added that a woman's destiny was to suffer and sacrifice. "Why so?" I asked. With all the seriousness she could muster while fluttering her recently painted fingers in the air, Farah said that I would learn soon enough. And then she said nothing more. She was too busy blowing her nails dry.

Farah's suitor, Jahan, and his family were already seated in Aunt Zarrin's living room. Pleasantries had been exchanged. Everything worth complimenting had been complimented, especially Aunt Zarrin's delectable potato quiche. Other trays of appetizers had made several rounds—perhaps too many rounds, for the piles of pits, peels, and shells sat high on the plates. With each pass of the tray, the air of anticipation in the room thickened. Now the only appetite left was for tea, and it could be delayed no more. Everything was ready: the sweets were on the plates, the boiling water was clamoring in the belly of the samovar, the little gold-rimmed glass teacups were standing spotless in their saucers next to the carved silver sugar cube jar. And everyone was waiting for tea or, truer yet, for the bearer of the tea, for Farah, to arrive.

Finally, holding a dozen brimming tea glasses on a silver tray, she appeared on the threshold of the living room. In her presence, the awkward mood in the room turned to one of awe. Farah looked exquisite. Her long honey-colored hair fell over her naked shoulders and arms. In her white strawberry-print dress, she looked more sumptuous than the strawberries. She wore a pair of red pumps with crisscrossing straps, which kept her freshly polished toes in place. It was now Farah's turn to be complimented. Jahan broke the silence:

"My dear Farah! You, you! Well, what can I say but . . . but . . . the poet says, 'I was longing for you to arrive, so that I . . . so that I . . .'"

Whatever the poet's thoughts were, he could not complete them. He had invoked "the poet," surely, to charm the family. But to engage in the national pastime, declaiming poetry, especially in the presence of an elder pro like Father, was foolish. He came to Jahan's rescue: "'So that I share my miseries with you. But alas, misery vanishes when you arrive.' Great choice, Mr. Jahan. Now we discover that you have literary talents, too."

Jahan cocked his head in Father's direction, his face beaming in the glow of undue praise. Farah blushed. All eyes in the room were on her, and despite the attention, she walked, with poise and a steady hand, held the tray before each guest, without a drop of tea spilling, and greeted everyone. To ease the pressure on Farah, Father put on his glasses and said, "Jahan had the right idea to start the evening with poetry," and reached for the mantelpiece. On it there would be a volume of Hafez's collected poetry, just as certainly as there was a flag in every schoolyard, equal tokens of patriotism, and he went on: "Let us see what Hafez has got to say about the future of our families."

Jahan's mother chimed in: "I don't believe in palm readings, tarot cards, or any other such mumbo jumbo. But Hafez"—she arched her eyebrows in deference—"well, Hafez is Hafez. He has never failed me once."

Then she asked Farah, whose tray was empty by now, to take a seat beside her. Aunt Zarrin, too, had to have a say about the legendary poet. So she went on to boast, "There's not a room in this house without a copy of Hafez. My husband just will not have it."

Passing his hand over the book, Father closed his eyes and recited the traditional incantation: "'O Hafez of Shiraz! Only you are the revealer of all secrets!'"

His fingertips ran across the edge of the pages several times. Creating suspense was an essential prelude to reading Hafez. "In the name of God"—he squeezed his eyelids, praying—"let Hafez of Shiraz guide us." And he repeated the words until his finger slid into a fold and he at last opened the book. Even for Father, declaiming Hafez flawlessly was not easy. In silence, he skimmed the lines. Jahan's mother asked teasingly, "Tell us, Mr. Hakakian, does Hafez think this is a good union for our two families?"

The room was hushed. Father finally began: "'You are the hyacinth, my beloved, to which every perfume owes its scent. You command so much, yet you do nothing but reprove.'"

Jahan said, "This is exactly how captivating I find Farah's beauty. And she spurns me. Oh, how she spurns!"

Farah blushed again. Jahan's mother tapped a hand on the back of Farah's hand to assure her that her son's hyperbole was indeed flattery. Father read on: "'You pass, lightly as the wind, over the corpse of your lovers, the martyrs of your love. But alas, your logic is the logic of time. You will not be detained, ever rushing forth.'"

Jahan said once more, "Every lover's predicament. The beloved devastates, but what are you to do but submit and sacrifice? Love torments and you abide. Cruel and endless suffering is all there is to love in a nutshell. Do I know Hafez or what, Mr. Hakakian?"

Father read on till he came to the last line of the *ghazal*: "'When will you ever cast a gaze Hafez's way? I long for it, even knowing that it ruins what it glances.'"

Aunt Zarrin protested, "Enough of this talk of ruin. It's a bad omen."

Father disagreed: "On the contrary. What Hafez is saying is that there is a man here tonight with love in his heart, determined to win over his beloved."

Everyone applauded. And so did I, my eyes fixed on Jahan. In Persian, Jahan means "world," a name into which he had surely grown. He looked gigantic. In Aunt Zarrin's living room he seemed to be sitting on the air itself, since the chair had vanished under his frame. He had one arm tight on the back of Father's chair while his other arm reached for the appetizers that marched past. His voice was colossal, too. His raucous laughter broke every silence. And what few vacuums his presence left unfilled, his garish manners filled. He had arrived in a boat of a Cadillac that barely fit Aunt Zarrin and Uncle A. J.'s alley. On the backseat, as he had told every guest that night, he stored an assortment of chocolates *just* for Farah, because someone had once mentioned she had a sweet tooth. If this was a sign of his dedication, it was lost on me.

The room fell silent again, and this time Jahan's sister broke it: "Have you done much traveling, dear Farah?" But she did not wait for Farah to answer. Jahan had trotted the globe and, according to his sister, spoke French, Hebrew, and English well. Hearing the word *French* got Grandmother's attention. In her Persian skin, Grandmother was an old, ailing matriarch. But in her French skin, she was sixteen and ebullient. Her lips, too, turned sixteen when she spoke French as she puckered them to say: *"Cela est merveilleux, monsieur. Avez vous également étudié à l'Alliance françaises?"*

Jahan drew a blank. He pulled a handkerchief out of his pocket to wipe his forehead, which did not need wiping. Then he threw down his head and muttered, *"Mashallah, mashallah!"* Father, on the verge of telling his favorite Hebrew anecdote, quickly refrained.

My dislike of Jahan did not all have to do with him. I was rooting for another man. Eavesdropping on Farah's endless telephone tête-à-têtes, I had learned that she had a flame: a penniless boutique salesman who allegedly resembled the heartthrob and pop singer Darius. The salesman's was the only call—ring once, hang up, and ring a second time—that she answered in a hoarse voice. To talk to him, she turned away from anyone who happened to be in the room. She focused her attention on a corner, any corner, while squeezing the telephone cord in her hand. Gravity, at those moments, pulled more forcefully at Farah. By "How is it going?" her knees had buckled, and whatever the next line, she said it lying on her side and twisting the cord past her body parts:

first her toes, then her ankles and calves, and finally her wrists and arms. When the cord reached her lips, the conversation had neared its end. This voluntary collapse of my cousin to the floor, followed by the far-reaching, superfluous, yet intractable twisting motion of the cord, I interpreted as the symptoms of love. Naturally, I wanted it to conquer all.

That night, when we were briefly alone again in her room, I asked Farah if she had fallen in love with Jahan. She said that of course she had not, but love was child's play, and she had become an adult. Jahan was a successful businessman who could give her everything she had ever wanted. Having been a witness to Uncle Ardi's ordeal, I wanted to speak up this time. To have the ear of an adult, I had to transcend my age. Using fancy vocabulary was how I hoped to achieve that transcendence: "The foundation of a felicitous marriage cannot be built upon material things."

Farah looked at me suspiciously and asked where I had learned this. I knew it had got her thinking. I also knew she would not care about it if I told her the truth. So I said that I had heard it from Mrs. Kamkar, my social studies teacher. Farah said nothing for a few moments and then sighed in resignation and asked, "How can I live without material things?" But as I had no answer to give, she dashed back to join the guests.

So I lied. It had not been a big lie, but it was a kind I had attempted for the first time: one that I had told not to save myself from the fury of an adult. On the contrary, I had lied to save an adult from making a childish mistake. My heart began to pound. Did my face show it? I stepped into Farah's spot before the mirror. I was unchanged. I blamed the mirror for my lie. The mirror had emboldened me, the way it always emboldened Farah. In it, I had seen to the heart of the dreamy girl who wanted her share of happiness. Standing where she did, I also saw what I was not: blond and fair. I was dark. I was not the one with the tiny upturned nose. Mine was huge with a bump on the bridge. I was not plump. According to my parents, I was "alarmingly thin." Sometimes Father, twirling my hand in his, held my wrist between his thumb and forefinger and asked disconcertedly, "What is this?" It was as if he were holding a twig that could easily snap. My limbs looked just as fragile. In the mirror, they appeared flat and shapeless. Even my hair, fine and straight, bristled with static at the touch of Farah's brushes. How could she and I both be girls? Her arsenal of makeup was no consolation. I lacked the patience to hold the end of a Q-tip and lightly dab, dab, dab. It required the taming of certain inner forces I had yet to tame, forces of which Farah often complained: "You don't have a feminine touch!" I felt clumsy and tiptoed around her so as not to chip her delicate presence.

But despite all our differences, we had this in common: We were the only girls in the extended maternal family. The women-to-be. Farah was well on the road, and I was trailing her. Her destination would be my destination. The women before us were Grandmother, Aunt Zarrin, and Mother. And where were they now? At motherhood, a place with suffering to the north, suffering to the south, suffering to the east, and suffering to the west. Motherhood was the only mark of their femaleness. I had watched Grandmother, Aunt Zarrin, and Mother long enough to know that grim geography. They served the family freshly cooked meals while they stayed in the kitchen and ate yesterday's leftovers. After the meals, the men slipped into their pajamas and napped. The women cleared the plates and swept around the bodies, like nurses in an infirmary tending to comatose patients. Pain was their closest companion. They welcomed it, grabbing the handle of a searing pan without mittens. If they cut themselves, they spared the call to the doctor, even the Band-Aid, and insisted, grimacing in pain, that all bleeding would stop with the steady application of pressure. Only the purple stain of iodine or the red trace of Mercurochrome told of the wounds they had suffered quietly. Mother's migraines came and went with just a tight scarf appearing and disappearing around her head. Otherwise she stood at the sink as she did every day and washed dishes in cold water. We must have lived in terribly dirty times, because the women were forever washing. Soapsuds were permanently lodged in the crevices of their rings. Grime dulled their jewelry, the way safety pins, holding the straps of their slips, diminished the allure of their lingerie. Their bras were depositories for banknotes and shopping lists, anything but a tender form. No matter how glamorously they dressed, something would be awry: a button missing, a bulky sweater covering a party blouse to protect their backs from a draft. Some worry, some dark thought always engulfed their faces and eclipsed their shimmering gowns. These expressions dominated their faces no matter how hard they tried to smile for the photographers, to leave a positive impression on the negatives.

Motherhood was a melancholy affair. Mothers were martyrs. Everyone knew it. And no one expected less of them. Men suffered and sacrificed themselves only in poetry for the sake of love. In real life, women were the ones to perform those legendary acts. The words that described a model woman were charged with muted stillness. *Demure* was the most spirited. The rest conjured lethargy at best: "So-and-so carries herself in an admirably *weighty* manner." And before I was told not to take *weighty* literally, it had already burdened me. "So-and-so's voice will not be heard past her eyebrows." Quietness was celebrated. And I began to keep so many cries of joy inside, I feared for my chest.

Every year on Mother's Day, the national radio broadcast this special message: "Salutations upon all mothers, the promised paradise is under your feet!" Mothers would be delivered to happiness only upon death. So they rushed the inevitable. In sickness, it was Mother who, fearlessly, leaned close to me, stroked me, and whispered, "May Mother never see your pain. May your aches leave your body and enter mine instead. May I die and never see you ill." All of five feet and two inches, she threw me over her shoulder, like a girl shawl, and carried me to the bathroom. When she ran out of words of affection, she recited poetry, those tributes to motherhood she cherished. Some I knew from my school texts, so I recited them along with her. The most rhythmic—one we both knew well—was a poem about a son in love, who was ordered by his beloved to cut out his mother's heart as the proof of his devotion. But running to his beloved, the boy hurt his foot against a rock, and the still-beating heart of his mother lamented: Alas, my dear son's foot is hurt! Alas, my dear son has taken a fall!

Mother woke me by gently shaking my shoulder. The taxi door was open. Father was paying the driver. I had fallen asleep in Farah's room, had missed the big dinner, and had been transplanted by one of my parents into the cab. Now the three of us were standing at Crown Prince Square. We walked the rest of the way through the back alley, Minoo Alley, behind the Polidor Cinema. To the dismay of the neighbors and City Hall officials, the alley's dark and narrow way was a nocturnal urinal for the patrons of the area watering holes. It was also a shortcut to our home, short enough to be worth the stench. I walked it by hopping over the wet streaks on the asphalt. Father's footsteps, punctuated by the sound of Mother's heels, echoed in the alley.

"You slept through the big news!" Mother said. "You are going to be a bridesmaid!"

"Whose wedding?" I asked.

"Farah's, of course."

"To Jahan?"

I meant to express shock but instead I asked a question to which I already knew the answer. Mother sensed my irritation. "What's wrong with him?" she asked.

"He's not handsome. He lies. He's ancient, ten, twelve years older than Farah. And she doesn't love him."

This time Father objected: "He's mature. And he's got a good business. He imports parts." And then he added ruminatively, "Car parts? Agricultural machinery parts? I forget. But he does well. Anyway, what's it to you? You're not the one marrying him."

What was it to me? It was a feeling, not yet a thought I could articulate. Still I insisted, "But it's wrong. She doesn't love him. This will have ruinous consequences!"

Father teased, "Helen, did you hear your daughter? *Ruinous consequences!* We're raising our own Hafez!"

Mother said in consolation, "Love will come with time. You'll understand when you grow up."

Adulthood was light-years away, but the wedding, in only three months, was far enough away for Farah to break off her engagement. Much could change in three months. I vowed that night to be by her side at every step. Now that I had learned to disguise my own opinions as those of my teachers, I could be the home-brand Dale Carnegie. Friendly etiquette was his domain; marital matters would be mine. I would weaken her resolve and strengthen her doubts with sound advice and smart aphorisms. I would be there to remind her of her hopes, her beauty, the gods, and the secret mortal she loved. I knew I could never match her golden reflection, but I would be her dark double, the voice of her dreams in her ear.

But there were my sixth-grade circumstances to consider. And Farah had a living to make. In the mornings, her brother drove her to Pharmica Inc., where she worked as a secretary two floors below the Asia Insurance Company. She filed documents, typed forty-five words per minute on the Persian typewriter at her left, and forty words per minute on the English typewriter at her right, all the while carrying on long telephone conversations with her best friend, Fariba. Fariba's siblings were already in America, and her parents were planning to immigrate soon. As these were their last days, the two girls spent as many afternoons together as they could. Some days they went to the Ice Palace to skate. Other days they took the bus to Jordan Avenue in northern Tehran, a ritzy district, where they browsed the windows of Bebe or the pages of *Burda* magazine for the new styles and sewing patterns. Farah spent most of her earnings on clothes, makeup, and costly concealers, which she insisted on using despite having flawless skin. Most evenings, Jahan turned up at Aunt Zarrin's door. In the kitchen, he dispensed his usual quota of flattery to her, telling her what a great cook she was or how he wished to call her "Mom" very soon, then took Farah to dinner. She returned, every night, unmoved. Still the wedding plans moved forward.

The weekends brought our families together, and the after-meal hours briefly scattered everyone, as each found a corner for a siesta. Farah cozied with a copy of the weekly *Today's Woman,* and I snuggled up to her. She scanned the ads first:

Neptune Gas Grill: Freedom from Fanning; Toshiba Rice-Cooker: Never Strain Again; Sayonara Sandals: Comfort for Everyone; The Iran National Automobile Manufacturers Present: Peykan, the Fruit of the Iranian Genius; What Is the Difference Between a Sexy Woman and an Azmayesh Refrigerator? The Sexy Woman Is Hot, Hot, Hot, and the Azmayesh Refrigerator Is Cold, Cold, Cold!; Rooster-Brand Chewing Gum: Cleans Your Mouth, Relieves Indigestion, Calms Your Nerves, Enhances Your IQ.

But she stopped turning the pages when she got to the title "Tell Me What I Must Do?" Every woman I knew read those columns. I did, too, though I never understood them. Every episode had a similar protagonist, a "gorgeous inexperienced maiden," who had just arrived in Tehran, to work or go to college. By the end of the third paragraph, she would meet a man, whom she would call a demon by the end of the fourth paragraph. They would plan to go somewhere—the beach, the park, the theater—and in all of those places somehow there was always a bed. And soon the story had ended, every one in the same way: the girl, in the nude, in the man's arms, and the time, no matter morning, noon, or evening, was always "too late." By this point the girl entreated the reader to guide her, tell her what she must do, help her find a way to undo the "horrid deed" that would for-ever sully the family's honor, and derange her father and broth-ers, if they discovered her.

"What deed is that?" I asked, admitting my ignorance to Farah at last. But all she told me was not to entertain disgraceful thoughts. Being pure, she said, was the ultimate virtue. And without elaborating anymore, she warned me that I must never play too hard in school, jump too high, or fall too low. *Why?* I would learn soon enough. She licked the tip of her thumb and turned the page, sealing the subject closed.

Buried in the magazine were the finer headlines, the news of an emerging breed: female, but not familiar. Each caption set a record, each photo grabbed the attention for the sheer novelty of an image never before seen. One photograph drew both our eyes at once. Its caption read: "Salutations upon Our Nation's First Female Welders!" Wearing a pair of goggles, a woman stood alone in a factory and held a rod in one hand and a torch in another. I was mesmerized by the burst of light between her hands. Farah contemplated her goggles as a new vogue in summer shades. There were other photos, equally astonishing. The words "Sky Is the Roaming Grounds of the Brave Iranian Girls" appeared above the picture of two helmeted women, standing in front of an airplane, their bellies swelling with parachute. Farah admired their overalls. I wondered how they could hear each other under those helmets. But the caption I liked best was "A Reactor Queen Is Born!" Neither Farah nor I knew what a reactor was. Still, we examined the snapshot with great pride. There stood Dr. Zohreh Abedinzadeh, the chief of the nation's atomic experts, surrounded by men in white coats.

But the photo I cut out and glued to the back of my social studies book was my all-time favorite. It was of Pari Khanom, the nation's first woman trailer driver. As she stood by her monstrous truck, holding the door open with one hand, one foot on the step, the other on the floor, she exuded a steeliness I had never seen in anyone. Yet she was biting shyly on her lower lip, just like a girl, like my friend Z. Pari Khanom was ready for anything the road might bring. A better, vaster road than the one Farah was on. A road onto which I encouraged her to take a detour: "You know, your photograph could be here someday."

"Mine? What have I ever done?"

"You're nineteen. You can go to the university. Become a big—"

"A big spinster?"

"You could be the first female beauty whiz!"

She shook her head in objection, but her grin gave away her hopes. She could picture it in her mind's eye. I was only telling her what the gods had in the mirror. All she needed to do was convince Uncle A.J. to let her break off the engagement.

Like most fathers, Uncle A.J. left the day-to-day affairs of his children to his wife. His duty was to work. His profession—a wholesaler of precious metals—was no secret once he flashed his sparkling smile. Uncle A.J.'s teeth twinkled in gold and silver. At a plant in the suburbs of Tehran, Uncle A.J. melted the old, unusable gold and silver his customers brought and recast it into ingots. The smoke of the kiln sat on him in layers throughout the day. By the time he arrived home at night, a brown bag in hand, he looked like a vagabond, except that in this vagabond's bag were the precious ingots he had made that day. With the gold and the silver, the family believed that Uncle A.J. melted his worries away. Ever calm, without a single gray hair on his fifty-year-old head, he had earned the nickname "Pacific Ocean."

But against Uncle A.J.'s serene bearing, calamity crashed the afternoon Farah announced she did not wish to marry Jahan. Instead, she said, she wished to go to America. Fariba was already there and quite happy. Farah wanted to do the same. Aunt Zarrin asked the question she had so many times before: What could a girl possibly want that Jahan could not provide? What could any girl want from a man but his name and his children? Farah did not know the answer, but she was certain that there was more to life, and she wanted all of it. And once she uttered the words aloud, her desire for it made her tremble. Tears welled up in her eyes. Aunt Zarrin's voice rose, though she was still trying to reason. Uncle A.J. sat, staring out the window, but he was growing tired of listening to his wife and daughter argue. He was a man of few words: What about the love of family? What of loving the father who worked like a dog, for her and her brothers' sake? Was this his thanks? What about sacrifice? Did she think he loved Aunt Zarrin when he married her? Did Aunt Zarrin? If she really was an adult, she would make a sacrifice. And once she did, she would find love. That was that! His had always been the last word. He turned to face the window again. Uncle A.J. preferred to see things outside his own life: the television, or even strangers. Aunt Zarrin's voice had adopted a softer tone, seconding her husband. Building a family was building love. What did Farah think? And Jahan had all the right qualities. She was about to enumerate them, but Farah cut her off. This unexpected tantrum surprised the three of them, even Farah herself. Every other word from her mouth was a "No!" Uncle A.J. was looking away. But one look at her husband's temples, rippling as he gnashed his teeth, and Aunt Zarrin knew the tide of fury was rising in him. He was devising a punishment for Farah, for he believed in its rehabilitative qualities.

Tough love was his motto. There had to be a limit to conversation, to letting a child, and a daughter at that, raise her voice. There had to be a line beyond which a girl knew she could not step. To draw the line he had in mind, he grabbed the silver sugar cube jar from the coffee table and hurled it at Farah. The cubes went flying into the air, and the jar hit Farah on the elbow. She fell to the floor, her eyes rolled to the back of her head, and her body went into convulsion. The spasms continued and grew even more violent, until at last she passed out.

By the end of that day, the doctors at the local hospital, considering the preexisting history of epilepsy on Uncle A.J.'s side, had diagnosed Farah with the disease.

"No good suitor would ever marry an epileptic girl," were the first words Aunt Zarrin whispered to Mother when she saw us at the end of the corridor of Farah's ward.

In her gown on the bed, Farah was so pale she appeared ethereal, almost sacred. Without makeup, her face looked translucent. On the pillow, her fanned hair made a halo. Her palms faced the ceiling, and each wrist was punctured with the needle of an IV line. When I greeted her, she only asked, "Why are you here?" and burst into laughter. How odd was that laughter, raucous yet mirthless. Her nose crinkled. Her eyes narrowed to two slits, as if she were weeping. When it ebbed, she asked where Mother was.

"In the hallway with your mother," I replied.

"They're wondering what to tell Jahan about this," she said, and her face billowed into more of the same laughter.

She was right. Even drugged on a hospital bed, Farah could read the minds of the women in the family. They had come together again to save another of their children. But their minds, trapped by tradition, never found liberating answers. Saving Farah meant saving her engagement. It meant finding a way to keep Jahan from knowing what had happened to her. It meant lying. They were weak and alone against the world, and their solutions, forged by fear, reflected it: They told Jahan that Farah had a severe case of the flu. Nothing that two weeks of bed rest could not cure.

Three months passed between the night that Farah, in her strawberry dress, bloomed in Aunt Zarrin's living room and the day of her traditional bridal shower. A warm female air circulated in the passageways of Grandmother's house on that day. Trays of appetizers passed hands. The music of everyone's favorite diva, Googoosh, was playing on the stereo. Unlike the men, who had gathered in the guest room, the women permeated the house. The crackling of pistachio shells and the whispers of gossip filled the air: who was dating whom, who was about to marry, who could not get pregnant, who suffered from what disease, and who was either dead or about to die. The guests stuffed their handkerchiefs with the white, almond-centered wedding candy that they then tucked away in their handbags for good luck. It was an occasion for the elders to welcome the new bride into their own midst.

In the evening, the men began to trickle into the courtyard. They stood in the empty space where the baby blue BMW used to be, and I could not help wondering how Farah's destiny might have changed if Uncle Ardi had not gone away. Would he have driven her away from the madness, till they all came to their senses? Or would he have whisked her off to a faraway place, where he was allowed to marry Neela, and Farah, no one.

Father joined the men. In his left hand, he held a whetstone on which he sharpened a large knife. Then came the bleating of the sheep that had grazed in Grandmother's courtyard all morning. Someone was dragging its leash, and soon everyone had circled around it. Father started to recite prayers as he held his hand over the animal's neck. The sheep's head twisted under the pressure of his hand. Then Father's other hand plummeted. The women ululated. The sheep started to convulse. A thick red line streamed down its neck onto its hooves and over the tiles of the courtyard, until it collapsed onto its side.

Every time I think about Farah's marriage, the image of the dying sheep comes to my mind: four hooves jerking violently in the air while two masculine hands press against its belly. Throughout the morning, the sheep had walked with deliberation through the flowerbeds, sniffing every leaf, nuzzling against every branch, as if eternity were its to waste. But now its hooves chased one another through the air. These hooves had not a moment to lose. The sheep's body shook in random spasms. Then it slowed, but the range of the semicircles its hooves still kept making widened. Then it stopped and the hooves drew one last arc in the air. The men took a couple of steps back but kept their eyes on it. Several spasms followed. Finally, its exhausted muscles began to twitch. Then it was still. Its eyes froze to a look of expectation of soon rising and running again.

The men moved closer. Someone turned on the hose to wash away the blood. The ground turned pink. Red seeped inside the ridges of the tiles, into the soil of the flowerbeds. The men squatted around the sheep. The corpse had energized them. They seemed in command. One of them put his mouth against a puncture in the sheep's skin and began to blow into it. The sheep bloated. Another sharpened a knife. Someone else kept rinsing the blood off the courtyard slate. A few, unable to find a task, instructed the others. Then the knife was lowered once more to make a cut over the sheep's belly, and a line was drawn from its neck to its tail. When the men tugged at the two sides, its skin peeled smoothly like a piece of fruit, as if it had been meant to come off. Blood had at last been shed. The festivities had been made official. Sacrifice had come, and so had death. Love was sure to follow now.

At 7:00 A.M. on the day after Farah's wedding, there was a loud knock on our door. Seconds later, I heard Aunt Zarrin whispering an apology to Mother in the hallway. "Forgive me, dear Helen. Forgive me." Her voice was grave. She seemed to be pleading for absolution.

Mother hushed her and guided her to the room behind mine. The divider that separated the two rooms was not fully closed. Through the opening, I saw Aunt Zarrin dressed in slippers and a misbuttoned coat. Half her head had kept the puffy wedding hairdo, the other half was flat. Such an unkempt appearance was very unusual for anyone related to Farah, much less her mother. Seated next to her sister on the bed, Mother asked if she wanted a cup of tea. No, she had no appetite for anything, and begged Mother: "Must go to the bridegroom hotel now. Come with me!"

Aunt spoke in broken phrases, which Mother tried to piece together. At first the fragments made no sense to her: "Farah and Jahan . . . in bed . . . deed done . . . the bloodstain . . . small . . . very small . . . too small . . . not enough at all . . . suspicions . . . Farah's virtue . . . ruin . . . the family's honor . . . ruin . . . ruin . . ." Mother asked her to slow down and repeat the story several times. Finally it was clear: After making love to Farah, Jahan became suspicious of her virtue. The size of the bloodstain, the proof of her virginity, did not satisfy him. Virginity, for Jahan, had a direct correlation with size, an appropriate standard for a misshapen behemoth like himself.

At dawn he had called his mother with the news, and she was on her way to the hotel. So was a forensic doctor who would examine Farah and the stain. Aunt Zarrin wanted Mother to go with her to be by Farah's side. Throwing one roaring fit, I planted myself in the cab along with the two of them.

After leaving the newlyweds, Aunt Zarrin and Mother walked the length of the hotel block without exchanging a word. They were going nowhere in particular, and I followed them. At the first major intersection, a cabdriver stopped and asked if we needed a ride. And so our aimless pacing ended. The orange taxi with its white top was the only cheerful sight I saw on that gray morning. I sat in the backseat between Mother and Aunt Zarrin. Legs and arms spread, they looked like two popped bubble gums splattered against the seat. They mumbled to themselves, at times intermittently, at times together, "Thank God for the doctor" and "How could they doubt poor, innocent Farah?" A scandal had just been averted. Mother wondered if a chicken should be slaughtered and given to the poor to mark the occasion of saving Farah's reputation. Aunt Zarrin promised to make a donation to the Jewish hospital in south Tehran instead.

Exhaustion followed their relief. They were dazed and mostly silent. The worst was over. Or so they believed. Jahan's suspicion about Farah's virginity, they concurred, was mere male jealousy.

It was years before they learned the truth about his mental insta-
bility, his case of severe clinical paranoia, and even more years till
they discovered that Farah's epileptic episode was only a transient
condition and that she had been misdiagnosed. That morning, the
women knew nothing of this future. They could not. They were
no fortune-tellers, and *that,* I understood. But I also understood
that they had failed to see what the past few months had shown
them about Jahan. They had even failed to see what the present,
that very morning in the bridal suite, was showing them. Of what
exactly had gone wrong, I was uncertain, and neither Mother nor
Aunt Zarrin would explain it to me. But I saw no hope of bliss
when Jahan and Farah's first visitor on the first morning of their
matrimonial eternity was a forensic expert.

These thoughts passed through my mind as the streets passed
before my eyes. The adults around me, frenetic creatures, had
done their best to stop one wedding from happening only to rush
another. The men I once thought of as a single entity had become
three distinct kinds: the penniless, who stood no chance; the
giants, whose proportions obscured clear view; and the calm and
the sweet-natured, who sacrificed good sense to tradition. All of
them had swaggered about women, vowing to keep them from
harm. All of them stood by and watched Farah be forsaken. Real-
izing this should have saddened or disillusioned me. But instead it
filled me with glee. The grown-ups could not tell fortunes, but I
could. The crystal ball was in my possession. I had seen what even
Father had missed.

The taxi made a turn onto Pahlavi Avenue, the city's main
artery. It was quieter than usual. Row after row of grooved metal
shutters covered the glass windows of the stores. It was Friday.
Shops were closed. A few kids played by the pool of Crown Prince

Square. Some were jumping rope. Two were drawing something on the ground in chalk. I did not wish to join them. I did not envy them. Never had I felt so alone, yet so content. I wanted to be home, reading. Reading made everything better, no matter what I lacked, no matter how strange or lopsided I seemed to myself. Some children wore braces on their teeth, glasses on their eyes, or special shoes on their feet. Reading was my corrective device. In books, I met people I admired. Like Helen Keller, I would heed my senses. Like Marie Curie, I would marry only a man like Pierre, soul mate, lab mate, who would truly believe in me. Now I understood why the Curies never kept more than two chairs in their living room, lest visitors feel too comfortable, extend their stay, and thus delay radium. Somewhere beyond my home, beyond my family, there had to be a bigger universe, a sea perhaps like the one the little black fish had fancied, with possibilities greater than the ones I could see, where women lived differently from those close to me. And I would read my way out to them. This was my secret. It did not need to be kept locked under a silly clasp because it was safe in my chest. This secret soothed me. Maybe being a girl detective was not my calling, as I once had thought. Years ago, I yearned to discover other people's secrets. But that was before I had secrets of my own. Maybe I was meant to be not just a girl, but something more, like an interpreter. A kid who could make sense of what puzzled others.

I scanned the graffiti on the street walls. The words on one of the storefront shutters read: "Nasrin Please Call Amir!" A telephone number appeared next to Amir's name. Several doors down there was another line, written in red and in a rush. Four ominous words: "Death to the shah!"

5

ON THE ROOFTOPS

WHEN I SLOWED TO CATCH MY BREATH ON THAT OCTOBER afternoon in 1978, I saw the two lines that had trailed me: One white, the other red. One of chalk, the other of blood, from my bleeding feet. I could not see the wounds. I felt no pain. Barefoot, I had walked for a kilometer, maybe more, with only the walls as my guide. Where could I go? Not home. My parents had dreaded this day. I had to be strong. Father's words rang in my ear: "When everything fails, write your way out of misery." But trying to keep my promise to him, all I had done was to draw a line, and even that was broken: perforated over the brick facades of apartments, and brittle over the terra-cotta surface of houses.

Our family had been halved. Mother, Father, and I were all the Hakakians left at number three Alley of the Distinguished. In September, Javid had entered the university as a freshman, and two days later, he found his way to the campus's anti-shah demonstration and an overnight detention by SAVAK. The next week, Father wasted no time arranging for Javid and Behzad to go to America. There was no banter this time. No one to jump on the traveler's back and whine. Anyway, there were more of us leaving now than staying, and it was hard to know who had to console whom. On the eve of their departure, I was afraid to go to sleep, lest I wake up a drowsy child again, unable to bid them a proper good-bye. I stayed up with my brothers and their friends, who pledged to fill in their place for the four-year interim, till they finished their studies and returned with their degrees.

Fog unfurled its coat along the street. Or was it dusk approaching? Time had slipped from me. And of space, I knew only that somewhere far behind was the school from which I had been excused that afternoon: "Roya Hakakian, report to the principal's office. Roya Hakakian, bring your belongings and report to the principal's office immediately." The voice of the assistant principal blared through the empty corridors while I packed and marched toward the principal. I could see his outline while he waited at his office door, at the other end of the hallway. The news he thought he was breaking to me was no news at all: my tuition payment had not been made. Father had not been able to cover the costs of Javid and Bez's travels and pay for the afternoon sessions at my school, too. For the remainder of the year, I could only attend the "public" portion of the school. The principal asked if I understood. I nodded. From then on, I, unlike others, would go home at 1:00 instead of 3:30 P.M. He hoped, rubbing his hands together as if to rub hope into being, I realized how sorry everyone was. I nodded again. But since I was such a strong student, no one worried that this would in any way affect my performance in the morning sessions. They were, after all, the only ones required according to the national standards and available to all free of charge. Mostly English was offered in the afternoons, and of what use was that anyway? He patted me on the back. His pity weighed on me. So I nodded a last time, asked permission to leave, and before he had granted it to me, grabbed a piece of chalk from the box outside his office and ran. At the entrance, I took off my sneakers, tied their laces together, threw them over my shoulder, and began walking.

The hardness of the chalk between my fingers, of the pavement beneath my feet, was the sensation I wanted inside. I wanted hardness to seep through my skin while Tehran's tenderness enveloped me. Tehran had never failed me: the music of water in the canals, the cry of the peddlers, the generosity of its vendors giving away a hearty sampling of cooked beets or fava beans to a lost girl. And to keep a lone passerby company, its walls stretched and stretched. They did so that afternoon, and my sadness ended long before the walls did, at the iron gates of Tehran University.

Being excused from that school in the afternoons was hardly a loss. It was a new school and I was unhappy in it. I had felt like an outsider ever since the year began. The afternoon classes had been designed for kids who spent their summers in Europe or America. They could recite old American fairy tales by heart, whereas my eyes, encountering English for the first time, were only beginning to adjust to the torrent of the alphabet that flowed across the wrong side of the page. At that moment, however alone, I felt relieved from having to win their friendships, relieved to have dodged English for what I believed would be forever.

The university block looked eerie. The street whose cafés, sidewalks, and bookstores always pulsated with browsers was desolate. This was where Uncle Ardi strolled to buy his afternoon drink. He came here because, even on the quietest afternoon, tearooms teemed with patrons. Their busy servers, towels over their shoulders, cigarette butts in the corners of their mouths, balanced several cups, saucers overlapping saucers on each elbow, and glided between the tables. Now the servers were sitting idle, steaming along with their samovars. The bookstores had closed but the owners perched behind the windows, eying the street. Other shops had lowered their shutters, but only halfway, uncertain whether to lure or refuse customers. The welcome sign on one side of the door undid the BACK IN A FEW MINUTES on the other side. The street was pondering a grand decision—to continue or not to continue with the business of the afternoon.

Was this the city I knew? A tire burned in the middle of the street. With the slightest breeze, ash and paper swirled and settled on the asphalt. A canister kept banging against the curb. Thick with smoke especially near the dying fire, the air felt like needles, piercing my skin and eyes, stinging my tongue. The porcupine air brought on a fit of coughing. The tears I had held back at school rolled down my cheeks in front of the university.

An army truck turned the corner, pulled to the middle, and parked sideways to block traffic. Wearing masks, a dozen soldiers stepped off the truck. One jumped on the hood and pulled down a banner of which I stole a blurred glance: *Down with . . .* The trail of the banner had curled at the end of the rope. The soldiers held their guns at their waists, divided into twos, and scattered through the grounds. They scuttled, stopped, and motioned to one another against the distant shriek of sirens and the chopper that hovered just above them.

"Hey, little girl! You lost?" whispered a student peering at the street from behind a tree. He was holding a rag to his face but moved it to say, "Don't stand in the middle of the sidewalk like that."

I stepped back and leaned against the middle arch of the university entrance. With inflamed eyes, I saw a few bruises on the arch's wall, and layer upon layer of posters. Toward its base, there was a print of a portrait in profile. It was of a mullah, for I could recognize his turban but not his face. Under his image, a line written in colored chalk read: "No one graduates here till the shah leaves!"

"Do you see any soldiers, little girl?" the student whispered.

I scanned the street but saw only two soldiers, their backs turned to me, guarding the truck. I shook my head at the tree. He snuck out and motioned toward the bushes behind him. His gaze fixed on the street, he spoke, as if to the street: "What are your sneakers doing over your shoulder?" He dusted himself and ordered, "Put them on! Don't worry about your eyes. It's tear gas. It'll go away by the time you get home. Where's your home?"

Raising my hand, I pointed to my right. He flashed an adult smile and said, "You've got to talk. I can't read an arm yet. I'm only a sophomore."

I did not smile, only said, "Crown Prince Square."

From under his coat, he pulled out a ream of flyers and threw them in the canal. Then he motioned toward the bushes again and three others shot up and ran. With his gaze still fixed on the street, he issued another order: "Put your shoes on and get away.

Are you a good runner? Run up in this direction and you'll get to Elizabeth Boulevard in a heartbeat. You get it, right? Go!"

On the corner of the alley, the Corpulent Cop was showing Zaynab an old sleight of hand. When she saw me, she shrieked, "Back so early—you sick or something?"

Seeing the pair was reassuring: the Corpulent Cop bored as always, Z restless for my return. Living four doors away from us, Z was my best friend in the alley. She attended a public school in the neighborhood and came home at one every day. But our rendezvous was set for four o'clock, after I came home from the extra afternoon hours. We both blamed English for keeping us apart but could only allude to our grudge. A few days after I had begun at my new school, she had asked, "So can you speak English now?"

"Very well."

"Say something, then."

And I recited the opening lines of "Sleeping Beauty," which I still could not read but whose sounds I had memorized: "'Whoance upon a time, there vas a king and a qveen.'"

Encore! She asked that I repeat the words so she could learn them, too. Confidently, I began instructing her: "You have to put your lips together like you're blowing bubble gum and then slowly, slowly, slowly let go. That's how you have to say *whoance.* You can't say it like a *v.* You have to go *whoa.* Whoance."

"Whoance!"

"And when you want to say *there,* you have to make like you're gurgling saltwater in the back of your throat. *Rrrrr.* It takes practice."

She put her hands at her waist, threw her head back, and gurgled until I stopped her: "And for the *th* in *there,* press your tongue to your teeth. It's really a *z* stuck in a *d*. If you want to say it like Americans do, you have to lisp."

"You stay all these hours extra in school to learn to lisp?"

But I would lisp no more. Z and I had every afternoon together now. Z was my age, tall and willowy like me, and I thought her beautiful despite her outdated name: Zaynab was a distinctly religious name—the name of the prophet Muhammad's cousin and wife. A name uncommon in the Alley of the Distinguished. Her name alone had alienated her from other kids in the neighborhood. But I saw it for what it was—only a name—and I loved her, for being what no one else was, a perfect playmate. In Z's eyes, the Alley of the Distinguished was a universe over whose stars I was the one who ruled. She played as I wished, followed me wherever I went, and believed me if I lied. When I made her swear to secrecy, then claimed to have superhuman powers, she did not laugh or doubt me. She only asked to watch me communicate with my extraterrestrial friends, who had endowed me with those powers. For days I kept saying that her request was being reviewed "up there," until at last we went to the rooftop, where, as we would soon learn, all kinds of divine pageantry took place. Sometime just around dusk, the tin cover of a neighbor's air conditioner looked ablaze in the reflection of the setting sun. Directing her attention to that flaming object (*flaming* sounded sacred to the Jew in me and the Muslim in her), I had shut my eyes, put my thumb and index fingers on my temples, assumed a grave look, and shushed her so I could register the celestial messages:

"A green Peugeot is about to turn into the alley." Mr. Soroudi always returned home around that time. "Your sister Bibi will do well on her next test." Everyone knew Bibi was a star student. To all the trifles I palmed off as magic, Z listened with earnestness.

On overcast days, we dived into the underbelly of Z's house, into the dank, windowless basement room the family called the "chest room." There was no other furniture in that room but a chest against its back wall. Sitting on the pile of blankets over the chest, we played Stone, Pappper, Scissssors! I slowed the words, waiting for Z's anxious hand to creep from the back of her head, revealing her intentions. Her bony fingers, with round, prim nails gesturing paper, remained frozen in the air, until my cheating scissors cut it in half. The chest room devoured us in a happy oblivion, where we hoped to stay till the kingdom come. But it could never come, because Mother always came first, looking for me: "Mrs. Banoo, may your shadow forever linger over your children's heads. Have you seen Roya? Roya! . . . Roya!"

Worry or fury never stood in Mother's way of first asking Mrs. Banoo to forgive the troubles I had caused—*what troubles?*—or hoping for Mrs. Banoo's exhaustion to abate speedily. When I surfaced, Mother gave me a hard look and shook her head in disappointment: "You know, Roya, everything has a limit. Playing has a limit. Do you understand limit?"

In a show of maternal camaraderie, Mrs. Banoo would give a gentle smack to the back of Z's head and say, "Enough playing, Z. Enough! You big lazy bear of a girl!"

That afternoon, I said nothing to anyone about the events I had seen in front of the university. We went to my home, where my mother asked Z, as always, if she was hungry, to which, like all other questions aimed to measure her desires, Z said, "No, thank you." A good Muslim girl, like a good Jewish girl, had to be demure and demand nothing. Z tried her best never to seem too eager for anything. But her constitution was made of flesh, blood, and restlessness. When she reached our door, her finger would not let go of the buzzer. Running inside, she nearly tripped, because her green Otafuku sandals with the plastic flower on the insteps, hastily put on, were always on the wrong feet. And when Mother finally served dinner, Z, while still insisting "No, thank you," grabbed the offered plate, sat cross-legged by my side, and ate ravenously. It was in the enthusiasm she could never tame, in her failures, in the wrong ways she appeared, in all the things our two families could not afford, that our bond had been formed.

Mother was a perfect cook; Z's mother, forever sour over having married a man thirty years older, was a mother perfectly absent. So we ate at my home and played at hers. But that evening, after barely a few minutes in the chest room, boredom set in. I confided to Z about my day. But she could only say what her father had told her, use the same word my father had used to describe the streets in those days: *noisy*. "Noisy," we repeated to ourselves, feeling the inadequacy of our fathers' explanation in the austerity of the word. *Noisy* lingered in the air until Z said she had a secret, too. Turning her back to the door, she lifted her sweater. "Touch here," she whispered as she gently pressed my fingers to her chest. "They both hurt. Do you think it's a tumor? Am I getting cancer?" It could not be cancer because I lifted my sweater to let her feel the answer.

In silence, my hand slid over her coarse, dark hair to her neck and followed the crumbs of her spine all the way down her back.

She draped an arm around my waist and breathed warmly on my face. Her lips against my cheek placed a kiss unlike any other before: drafty, soundless, deliberate, dizzying, but not in a sickening way. Our legs shifted to a new gravity—not under but between us. We slid closer and nested our legs on top of one another. There were no screams, no words, only a gentle thrill, without our usual pandemonium.

As the plume of breath grew over us, the sound of Z's uncle's footsteps came. And then his voice: "Allahu-Akbar! Allahu-Akbar!" In making His intrusions, the great God was above timeliness. Z and I listened. No one feared Great-Uncle. He did not look at the world unless he had to, and even then, only with a squint to expose himself to as little of it as possible. Great-Uncle was the only truly observant Muslim I knew. He was all the Islam I knew: an old, scruffy man, living in the basement, benign and irrelevant to the life on the ground floor. Z's family loved him above all for the allowance he dispensed to the six children every Friday, without demanding anything in return. Persian was his language, like it was everyone else's. But one would never know that by listening to him. He followed the orders of Mrs. Banoo to fetch bread three times a day. In the mornings, she hollered at him once: "Great-Uncle! Chop, chop. Two *barbaris* for breakfast."

But to every Persian request, he replied with some religious incantation in Arabic: "Allah o ma sal-e ala Muhammad va al-e Muhammad."

And so he would deliver a *salavat,* a salute, to the prophet Muhammad and all his kin. That much Arabic even I understood. Between two loaves of *barbari* breads, between every routine and the heaven, Great-Uncle always found a link. In all seasons, he shuffled around the neighborhood in a buttoned-up shirt and black pants under a brown robe. The backs of his shoes folded under his heels, laces never tied, he would not bother with the tedium that earthly footwear required. Had it not been for the unpredictability of Mrs. Banoo's occasional demands for a box of melba toasts, the neighborhood could have set its clocks by his daily traffic: 7:00 A.M. in the direction of the *barbari* bakery; 11:45 A.M. in the direction of the *taftoon* bakery; 7:20 P.M. Great-Uncle, somber as usual, holding a foot-long triangular *sangak* bread in hand, looked like a lone musician whose instrument had lost its sound.

"You back?" Z's mother called out upon his return.

"Allahu-Akbar," he shouted. God was indeed great. But at that time of the evening, when he was on the verge of missing his nightly prayer, that last praise of Allah was a plea: either to her to leave him be or to God to save him from her. Then the excruciating scratch of his shoes, dragging across the courtyard, faded under the sound of water gushing out of the garden hose, as he performed the ritual washing of his hands. Z and I listened to the pipes kicking and water rushing through the ceiling. Then the shoes dragged once more till they reached the basement, where he took them off to enter his room, next to the chest room. We held our breath. By the time his footsteps ceased, our embrace had come undone. The tangled mass of our bodies split in half, each into a corner, cooling in darkness.

When I peeked into Great-Uncle's room, often I saw a folded man: an ass resting on two cracked, grubby heels, under a rounded back. Then the back straightening, pausing in midair and bending once more till his forehead touched the prayer stone, a tan rectangle with the feel and the size of a bar of soap. Then he rose to his feet as his knees cracked and his robe jammed and unfolded to his motions, each punctuated by a string of whispers. His arms were before him, his palms turned in, as his voice broke in a whimper, a sob even, at times assertive, but always reverent. Great-Uncle did not pray to God. He bargained with Him over highly critical matters. And though he prayed five times a day, the intensity of his performance never waned.

For days after my banishment from school, one o'clock remained an uneasy hour. With each passing day of that autumn, outside the windows of the classroom, the snow fell and fell and it buried everything but my anticipation. The moment the bell rang, I reached under the bench, packed my book bag, and with it in one hand, lopsided and hunched under the gaze of everyone, I walked out. What sadness I carried with me lifted the moment I saw an alabaster dot in the horizon. With each leap I took toward it, the dot grew larger, until at last I stood, erect and elated, at its threshold—at number ten Alley of the Distinguished, at the door of Z's home.

Every day at one, the neighborhood slipped into languor. The peddlers disappeared. The long brooms of the street sweepers leaned idly against the walls. The traveling trash lodged itself between the rocks of the water canals. From window ledges where the strings of the open blinds used to reach, tails of drowsy cats dangled. The one o'clock air was bright, but the mood had the black quiet of after midnight. Z and I stayed awake, tiptoeing through the house, to study the rhythms of the afternoon. One-thirty pulled the eyelids over Z's father's eyes, glued his chin to his collarbone, and spread the newspaper across his lap. One forty-five silenced the creaking cribs of Z's twin sisters, and their breathing duet began. Two o'clock snuffed out the last flicker of Great-Uncle's murmurs. Two-thirty and 2:45 welcomed Z's brothers, Reza and Ali, on their bicycles into the courtyard. But three! Three opened the gates of whimsy. Through the cracked opaque glass ceiling of the attic shower stall, Z and I saw what would have seemed only a dream, if the steam of it had not dampened our cheeks. At three Z's eldest sister, Bibi, undressed to take a shower.

Until three o'clock, that splendid hour, Z and I had thought our reedy limbs were destined to become the varicose, stretch-marked limbs of our mothers. We had never seen or imagined a third female stage, until Bibi's hands circled around her back and undid her soaking bra, then reached down and rolled the elastic waist of her panties over her buttocks, thighs, knees, shins, till they dropped to the floor and she stepped out of them, perfectly nude. Bibi was that sublime possibility of which no one had ever spoken. Seeing her excited us for the first time about our futures. It also riddled our minds with questions: When were we going to grow into such beauty? Did we need to prepare? Would we look similarly exquisite or was that a matter of luck? We felt the smoothness of her curves by the way water behaved in her company: it was in no rush. It glided over her body with the slowness of a liquid of respectable density. How long before our clumsiness yielded to such poise, especially under such slippery circumstances? How long until we could balance one foot against a tiled wall and draw an endless line from the tips of our toes all the way to our hips with a razor? But first, how long until we would need a razor? She kept her eyes shut while her body turned and turned under the water, and we wondered: How many revolutions until we arrived at the hemispheres of such breasts? Of only one thing were we certain: this metamorphosis could not happen but overnight.

In the secret underworld of three o'clock all my despair was washed away. The mornings passed in reverie as I spent every hour dreaming of the afternoon, of that other school, at a home in a cul-de-sac. Watching Bibi, I watched my childishness swirl down the drain under her feet. How immature our games, how silly our curiosities had been. Behind the door of the stall, I left the miseries that seemed petty now. I left even my family. Bibi was my only way out of childhood. Only through Bibi, the beauty in private, the high school star, could I get to thirteen, a year that was a world away. To grow up to command the respect of everyone, I had to know Bibi. Adulthood was independence. And I would not be independent unless I made my own discoveries. Bibi was my own discovery.

For Z and me, talk had lost its allure. Now, only touch interested us. Every afternoon we lay on the chest and examined each other's bodies to see if our legs, our torsos, our arms, our hands were any closer to that female hour. Beyond the few glimpses we caught of her, Bibi was out of our reach. She roomed with Mrs. Banoo in the back of the house, where her dour mother would have no occasion to run into her husband. For Mrs. Banoo, Bibi was more than a daughter. She was what enabled her to tolerate her unhappy marriage. They spent the afternoons together, cooking, talking. And as we did not dare disturb Mrs. Banoo, we retreated to the chest room and filled the gaps in our knowledge of our heroine, what Bibi was thinking or doing, with thoughts of our own.

Luckily for us, that autumn Bibi began a daily descent into the basement. She came to visit Great-Uncle. At first Z and I thought

Bibi was in trouble and was confiding her problems to her uncle. His room was the family's confessional. They came in, sat across from him, and talked to his bald head, for Great-Uncle's eyes would be fixed on the carpet. But Bibi did not come to share her secrets. She greeted him, then took a couple of spins around the room to show the affection she could only express by the touches she put to the room. She took charge as if the space were her own: shook off Great-Uncle's prayer rug, folded and placed it on the mantelpiece, inspected his closet for what needed washing, and as the room was spartanly furnished, found little else to do. At the end of her tour, she straightened the only frame on the wall. It was a portrait of Imam Ali: his gentle, dark eyes, cast to one side, were set below a uni-brow, above a considerable mustache and beard. Behind his head, a gilded sun shone. His bust was wrapped in layers of emerald robes. A shy smile adorned his lips, which would have completed a pleasant image, except my eye always caught sight of the rosy blood dripping from the shining blade of the sword at his waist.

After this prelude, Bibi and Great-Uncle sat cross-legged on the floor, inches away from a cassette player—the room's only luxury. They came together not to talk but to listen. Great-Uncle scrambled through a box of cassettes, chose a tape, blew the dust off the cover, and inserted the tape into the deck. Then he said a few words to Bibi, which we could not hear, and pressed the play button. As Great-Uncle had to strain to hear, and leaned further into the speaker with every passing minute, Bibi began to raise the volume. Now we could hear intermittent pops, and the scratchy flow of air, and then, vaguely, a voice. Our ears slowly adjusted, and Z and I began to hear a man giving a speech—the same man, day after day. His voice had the accent of the poorly educated, drawls of the country dialect. The words were in Persian, but their meaning eluded us. The sentences were awkward: prepositions misplaced, pronouns singular in one line and plural in the next. Arabic words reared their heads among a Persian crowd. The speech did not have the melody of everyday Persian. At first it was boring, repetitive, like a lullaby. But being irreverent, and contemptuous, it kept us alert, and listening. The sentences circled onto themselves; the same words, the same phrases were repeated over and over, each time with only a slight shift in inflection, until they built to a crescendo and suddenly another sound rose, like a covey of pigeons cooing. It was of an audience crying.

Hearing the sobs, Great-Uncle rocked to and fro and dabbed his eyes. Bibi did not move. Her damp hair glistened, no matter how dimly the room was lit. The voice on the tape escalated to subdue the sobs, which were growing louder with the passing of every second. Now it issued rage, and the rage, in turn, provoked the crowd to weep even harder. That voice conducted an orchestra: it motioned them with a phrase. Cries rose. With a tiny change in pitch, it motioned again. The audience bawled, howled, "Allahu-Akbar!" The voice assumed an imperative tone, commanding the crowd. The cries heightened into chaos, all melding into a frenzy of pleas, chants, and sobs. Slowly we began to hear parts of the speech:

This world is but a passage. It is not a world in which we ought to live. This world is but a narrow path. What is called life in this world is not life but death. True life is that offered only in the hereafter. We are here, in this low, earthly life, only to perform the duties Allah has set for us.

We have not risen to secure positions of authority and become a government. We have no objective other than saving the oppressed from their oppressors. All that made me accept the leadership of the community is Almighty God's instruction that the clergy should not remain silent in the face of greed and the crushing hunger of the downtrodden. The shah is saying that he is granting liberty to the people. Hear me, you pompous toad! Who are you to grant freedom? It is Allah who grants freedom. It is Islam that grants freedom. What do you mean by saying "We have granted you freedom"? What has it got to do with you, anyway, to grant us anything? Who are you, anyway? Leave this country and go get yourself another job, you inept cipher . . .

One afternoon when Great-Uncle left on an errand in the middle of a speech, Bibi, who had caught us eavesdropping, waved us inside. At last we were in her presence, albeit in a dank room. She said, "Do you know what we were listening to?"

Z and I shook our heads.

"This is Agha speaking. You don't know Agha?"

We shook our heads even more emphatically.

"Agha is the one who'll set us free. What did you think? That things will stay the same forever? Agha is the angel who'll chase the devil away. Remember your fifth-grade Persian textbooks? The famous *ghazal* by Hafez you had to know by heart—'The devil shall flee and the angel shall arrive at its heels'? Hafez knew way back then Agha would be coming."

She recited those verses again through the end: "'. . . and a time sweet as sugar will follow!'"

Having watched Bibi for so many afternoons without ever talking to her, I was thrilled to be in a room with her, listening, even if she was making no sense: "Agha will divide bread and smiles equally among us. He'll not have cronies like that evil shah. He'll treat us all the same. The rich drive their Mercedes, take fancy trips to places you couldn't even find on a map. Their kids aren't any smarter. But they can afford tuition to the best schools, and the best tutors. You understand that, Roya, don't you?"

There was a look of mercy in her eyes. I turned to Z. She shrugged and said, "Was it a secret?"

My answer would have been a resounding yes, if we were not in the same room as Bibi. But I threw my head back, linked my hands behind my head, two fashionable gestures of equanimity, and said that it was okay. Bibi was not finished: "Sure, it's okay for you, because your dad can teach you everything. What about others? So many people suffer, just so a few can have cushy lives. A revolution is on the way. Agha will make poverty history. We'll be free to say and write anything we want because when Agha comes, SAVAK will also be history, too."

From the kitchen on the second floor, Mrs. Banoo summoned Bibi. Before rushing to her mother, she made one last promise: "If you keep your mouths shut, I'll tell you more. You never heard about Agha. Mum's the word!"

That night I lay in bed with my eyes open to my first full-blown insomnia. Calm had enveloped me. "Fair," "afford," "justice" had strengthened me. Over the rift in my days, these words had made a bridge: between the misfit in the morning and the covert marine observer of the afternoons. Old mysteries would finally be unraveled. SAVAK had resurfaced, and this time I already knew more: it was evil, and Bibi's angel would destroy it. I had yet to know who Agha was, or how he was going to make so much history, or what Bibi's revolution meant. But I was for it. In spite of all the ambiguity, I felt the certainty of an irrevocable change. While Bibi spoke of her angel's coming, she had become a heaven to me. Sometime at the end of this thought, sleep overcame me.

The next day, Bibi came down to Great-Uncle's room but kept her back to the chest room. All we could see of her was her sweater, which rode up to reveal the small of her back. We also saw her hands. They kept reaching for the dark mass of her hair, twisting it round and round as if she were to put it in a bun, but then letting it loose again. Half an hour passed without a sign. And I worried that, like her hair, she had started with the two of us only to let go. When Great-Uncle left on an errand and she still did not turn toward us, I went into the room. She looked distressed to see me there. She put her head down, looking at her lap. It was a look of regret, perhaps for having opened up to us the day before. But I was prepared to prove myself worthy of her trust. I reached under my shirt, took out *The Little Black Fish,* and told her, "SAVAK hates this book. My brother told me never to take it out of the house or show it to anyone."

She was intrigued, because she was looking up again, and her eyes flashed with yesterday's light. She asked how I had come by it. More confident now, I boasted that it had once belonged to my brother, but he was in America now, so for all practical purposes, the book was mine. Did she know it, I asked, for if she did not, I could tell her the story, which I knew by heart. I could recite it to her, page by page, if she wanted. Finally, a dimple on her cheek showed. She spoke: "This book is my all-time favorite. I know it well. But do you know what SAVAK did to the man who wrote it?"

"He was from Azerbaijan. It's in the northeast of Iran. You freeze there."

"So you think he froze to death?"

"I . . . well, no. But he wasn't sick, you see. Or old."

"That's it, then. You don't really know what this book is about."

"I do. It's about a little black fish that wants to go to the sea."

"So what?"

"Well, it's a stubborn little fish."

"And?"

"It doesn't listen to what its elders tell it."

"You've read the book, Roya. I give you that. But you really know nothing."

"Yes, I do. The little fish disobeys its elders and goes to the sea."

"And if that's all there is to this book, why would your brother tell you not to show it to anybody?"

She had a point. Javid had never explained to me why the book had to be kept at home. I was so pleased that he had shared an adult secret with me that any question, even the smallest probing, seemed like a betrayal of that trust. So I had not asked the obvious.

I stared at Bibi for a while, buying time in her gaze to come up with an answer. But she spoke before I did: "SAVAK killed him, you see."

"What's SAVAK?"

"The shah's secret police. They snatch you away, torture you, even kill you if you say something against the shah. That's what they did to the writer of *The Little Black Fish*. They put his feet in a block of cement and dropped him into River Aras in Azerbaijan."

"Cement? Building cement?"

"Yep."

She knocked on the wall and continued: "This, right here. Stuck his feet in cement and waited till it got hard so he couldn't move even a toe. And when they threw him into the river, he couldn't swim to shore. That's how SAVAK drowns people. He had said too much in his books. You and I are little black fishes who need to leave home."

"Go where?"

"I don't mean leave leave. I mean question. Protest against the pelican. Remember the pelican? That's the shah. That's SAVAK. We're the fish. Everything is a symbol."

"Agha, too?"

Finally a smile brightened her face, and she said, "Agha is as real as can be. Agha is Ayatollah Ruhallah Khomeini. Hear the name? Ruh-Allah. The spirit of God! He has ordered everyone to go up to their rooftops at the stroke of nine tonight and shout 'Allah-o-Akbar' for ten minutes. We're all doing it."

The night chased Great-Uncle out of the basement and into the courtyard. The moon was full. He pointed to the sky. Several times he rocked moonward, and a few whispers shook off him along the way. Then he faced everyone standing in the courtyard. His cheeks and lips contorted first to an expression of pain, then surprise, until they slid into the forgotten shape of a smile and he uttered the only Persian words I ever heard him say: "By the grace of God, Agha's face is in the moon."

Speaking a language almost lost to his memory seemed to be a great effort for him. His lips opened wider than his usual mutterings required. Only then did I see what very few teeth he had. His mouth was old, but his feet had suddenly gained a youthful sprint as he charged toward the stairs.

Mrs. Banoo asked Bibi where in the moon she saw the image of Agha. Bibi took her mother's hand in hers and drew the outline of his face in the air. My eyes followed their hands, yet all I could see was some dark shadows on the right of the moon and a bright spot on the left. Mrs. Banoo was puzzled. Bibi insisted that the face was in profile and that the dark, bulky shadows on the lower right of the moon made his beard and the bright spot on top was his turban. Slowly, the shadows shifted and I, too, saw a profile with eyes cast down.

Great-Uncle stepped on the staircase. He grasped the banister. At each step he stopped, caught his breath, and panted a blessing. It was a beatific ascension: the holy man had emerged from the forgotten crevices of the house and was aiming for the roof.

At 8:45 P.M. the lights in the homes began to go off one by one. By 8:55 P.M. not even the night was as dark as our neighborhood. All but the heavenly bodies had heeded Agha's message. Under the full moon, the antennas and the tin chimneys emanated a silvery glow, enhancing the majesty of the dark. Nothing hung from the clotheslines, not even pins. The neighbors were on balconies and rooftops, even those with no intention to chant. And that was just what Agha did: he dazzled even his enemies by the power of his spectacles. Darkness had rendered all faces immaterial. The eye could see only the outlines of the crowd: some short, others tall, some hunched, a few seated— those were the cynics waiting to see if the night would compel them to join. For the first time since I knew Z, her family had come together in one place: Great-Uncle next to Mrs. Banoo, who stood beside her husband, each holding one of the twins. Z's brothers tossed a rock in their hands. Bibi rested an arm on Z's shoulder. This was Agha's first miracle: a family reunited!

And my family? I hopped over the dividers between the rooftops and joined my parents. Father was repeating under his breath: "Helen, do you see this? For as long as the eye can see. One stinking mullah can do all this?"

To commit what was memorable to mind, Father always needed Mother as witness.

"Shhh," she said, elbowing him, as if he had mentioned SAVAK.

He teased her: "Try to say *'Allahu-Akbar,'* Helen, or we'll risk irking the goyim."

Could *I* say *"Allahu-Akbar"*? The words echoed in my mind, but I could not utter them. "Say it," I urged myself, "one, two, three." But I could not. I had never had to say words in Arabic, to chant in a language other than my native Persian. I had never been expected to sound like a Muslim. Must I choose? My heart was fluttering in my chest and everywhere else. Excitement pulsated in my ears. It throbbed in my belly. I feared something unknown. I was brimming with the thrill of something unknown. My parents were scared, while no one around us seemed to be. Z signaled me from the distance, inviting me to join her family. And I found myself torn between staying on our rooftop or going to hers. Suddenly I envied Z, who was standing among her siblings. I envied their togetherness, their certainty, their eager anticipation for nine o'clock to strike.

At 8:57 P.M. two rocks struck the bulbs of the light poles at each end of the alley. The skitter of the shards against the asphalt in an alley so hushed sounded like a thousand glass bottles shattering. No one said a word. At 8:58 the Alley of the Distinguished stretched like a common alley, dark and desolate. But at nine o'clock it came to life. Moans of *"Allahu-Akbar"* billowed through the night. They were not orchestrated sounds but fitful, scattered through the alley. They rose as if every person's throat had been clutched. Their chests heaved with each breath: *"Allahh-u-Akbar. Allahhh-u-Akbar."* Each *Allah* expanded in the windpipes, inhaling air as if it were rapidly running out. For every gasp, a hundred more echoed in sympathy. The *Allah*s drawled longer with each chant—*h*'s barely fading under the *Akbar*s, until all fizzled into a single *Allah;* greatness slowly sundering, then dissipating in the intoxicated throats. The cloud of a single plea plumed over the alley. By 9:08 the plea was a desperation reverberating in His name. *Allah,* and not another word. *Allah,* and it sealed all the untold.

With every home a heap of kindling, the alley was a bonfire. Phantom flames had scorched the neighborhood. A thick, sonorous smoke hovered over every home. Every man, every woman, every child was burning: everyone a victim, everyone an arsonist.

6

THE BIG BANG

"GET READY TO PINCH YOURSELVES!" UNCLE A.J. BELLOWED, and lowered the gunnysack on his back to Grandmother's dining table. We had all gathered around the table, silent and intrigued. He flashed his bejeweled smile, a foreshadowing of what was to come. This was the third and last sack. They lay large and mysterious, begging to be opened. Standing at the head of the table, Uncle A.J. tucked his shirt, rumpled by his exertions, back in his pants and repeated, "Get ready, I tell you!" And with his fingers, caked with ash, he began to tug at the sacks' bottom corners. Several chiming sounds came. Then caressing the length of one sack, he ran up and loosened the twine around its neck. But the knot was too tight, a hitch in his performance. Bending over the sack, he bit into it, gave it a cross-eyed look, and pushed one end of the twine up through the loop. It came undone. When he had opened all three, he carefully laid the frayed pieces side by side. This was his final delay before the inevitable, before he bellowed one last time, "Close your eyes!" We did. There came a sound of jingling and three consecutive melodious downpours. "Now, open!" And when we did, we were all pinching ourselves.

There, on the table, the Tutankhamen treasure of Tehran was shining before us. Three mounds of gold, silver, and precious stones glimmered so electrically that we all took a step back. To reach and touch any of it was to believe that such a sight could exist outside storybooks. On Grandmother's antique dining table, however old, so breathtaking a feast had never laid—of chokers, lockets, bracelets, amulets, bangles, crowns, and tiaras. There were far more colors and shapes than I could name, but I could only recognize pearls, rubies, diamonds, and emeralds among them. Like a victorious bandit, Uncle A.J. said, "Roya, set the table with these!" pointing to a mass of flatware embossed with the peacock throne. "Tonight we'll eat like kings."

He poked at the pile, turning over an amber and ivory earring for Grandmother's inspection. She rocked from side to side in disbelief, and asked Mother to close the curtains. Then A.J. addressed Father: "How many times did I tell you teaching is no future? I tell you now, Hakakian: Quit tomorrow and I'll make you a millionaire by April."

He raised the middle and index fingers of his right hand in front of Father's face and issued his ultimatum: "Don't give me two years. Just two months. Starting tomorrow, first of February, till the end of March of this year, 1979. If I fail, I'll change my last name to MacJackass. Or whatever else you want. You're the poet. You'll find a title."

Gazing on the pile, Father murmured, "God help us, A.J. Where did you get these?"

"Robbed the treasury, that's where. Robbed the shah's and the palaces of his every crony, where else? It's here now and it'll be here for a very short while. You'll do what I'm telling you, if you're half as wise as your reputation."

"You can't steal, A.J. I know you."

"I didn't say I *stole,* but those who did brought the goods to me. Chance of a lifetime, Hakakian. Chance of a lifetime."

"Those who did" were the demonstrating crowds. No longer specters on rooftops, or disembodied howls in the dark, the revolutionaries had descended onto the streets in broad daylight. The city was under martial law. Schools and universities had been closed for weeks. Life in Tehran had come to a halt, yielding to make way for the angry demonstrators. No one worried about how the months of work stoppage or loss of productivity would reflect on them in the future. After all, there was rage, which in 1978 was not considered just a feeling, but a highly regarded occupation. Sacrifice was all the skill, all the experience it required. And poetry, no longer simply an art, was the official language of that rage, of the revolution.

Poetry . . . ah! Poetry had made Jahan's courtship with Farah official. With poetry, Tehran's courtship with the revolution became official, too. Late in the previous October, the city's intellectuals had staged "Ten Nights of Poetry." Sixty-one of Iran's best-known literati appeared on the stage of the Goethe Institute, and in ten nights, they recited 218 poems. Each poem alluded in some way to the shah's censorship. The poets did not slaughter a sheep, but there was plenty of blood. With 275 mentions of the words *blood, bloody, bloodied,* or *blood-red,* the city's elite galvanized the thousands in the audience for that great hour of the royal beheading—the dethroning of the king. By the tenth night every poet and every fan had resolved to drive *crown* from the lexicon. (After a careful review of both courtships later in life, I have come to believe that mixing poetry with bleeding brings grave consequences.)

In the hope of remaining on the throne, the shah drove his own men away. For thirteen years, the nation had known only one prime minister: Amir Abbas Hoveida. But to quell the rebellion, the shah ordered the arrest of Hoveida. Where was Coco now to revel in the downfall of his nemesis? The prime minister's first replacement resigned that same year. General Azhari made the mistake of referring to the chanting millions on the rooftops as "very few people with too many cassette decks." He, too, was forced out. Shahpur Bakhtiar had hardly begun his term when the demonstrators derided him as an opium addict, who would do best to retire and smoke in peace.

By September 1978, kerosene lines had begun to form. The strike of the antishah workers of the National Oil Company in the south had created a severe shortage and paralyzed the economy. At the kerosene distribution center around the corner of the Alley of the Distinguished, a sizable crowd stood on queue. By December, the owner of the center had to tie a rope to the doorknob of the entrance and loop the rope through the handle of every kerosene container to prevent customers from fighting over their space in line. The rope snaked past our door, past the Pahlavi Foundation, perfectly desolate now, and vanished in the horizon. The queue became a place to congregate and exchange the latest news. The customers blamed not the workers but the shah for the oil short-age, and cursed him even when the seasoning in their homemade sandwiches was not to their liking. The customers blamed the shah for all wrongs: the poverty in south Tehran, the lack of an open press, the devastating earthquake that year in Tabas, power outages, the single-party system, the illiteracy among the poor, the cold in the north, and even the colds in their chests. Every sneeze now invoked a "Bless you" and a "Damn that shah." "Down with the shah" graffiti adorned every wall. Gone were the royal titles, the Pivot of the Universe, the King of Kings, the Royal Possessor of Kingdoms, and the Shadow of God. All of his majesty's greatnesses had been reduced to one: the royal nose. Mohammad Reza Shah Pahlavi was now exclusively called "Mohammad the Nose." The army imposed an even harsher martial law in a last effort to restore the old order, but on January 16 the shah himself fled, "on a short vacation." His departure ended more than 2,500 years of monarchy, which was announced in two words: "Shah Gone!"

The shah's closest associates also fled, abandoning their homes to looters who found their way to an overnight fortune, which made its way to Uncle A.J.'s casting plant in the suburbs of the city, where he melted the stolen heirlooms into indistinct ingots. The mob could not keep the raided valuables for long, nor did they trust a fellow Muslim with the secret of their goods. A hefty sum, a smooth operator like Uncle A.J., and a good dose of "Jewish abracadabra" took care of everything that needed taking care of.

There were no fancy meals on an ordinary weeknight at Grandmother's home. But I set the table with all the gold-plated utensils, even the oyster forks, their sinful nonkosher associations overlooked. It was a most elaborate table for a meal of scrambled eggs and a side of cucumber and yogurt. Dressed in their house gowns, Mother, Grandmother, Aunt Zarrin, and Farah each put on matching sets of earrings, necklace, bracelet, and ring. Farah forsook the ring because none would fit on her finger——enormous in her ninth month of pregnancy. And I, in jeans and T-shirt, resisted everything but the platinum tiara with the splashes of freshwater pearls.

Holding an *AH*-monogrammed spoon in hand, Uncle A.J. boasted that he was about to eat with Prime Minister Hoveida's very own. Father disagreed. He argued that Hoveida was too modest a man for such frivolity and was languishing in prison not for those asinine charges of corruption, but for a charge no one was bold enough to state: being a member of the Baha'i religion, the most persecuted religious minority among Iran's Shiite majority. Uncle A.J. retorted, "They'll come for the Jews next. As for myself, I plan to make all I can and escape this dump as soon as I can. Los Angeles, here I come! By then I can afford to hire my own angels, 24/7."

His confidence high as his pile of jewels, he warned Father, "You do the same, Hakakian! You don't think your sons are safe to return to this mess, do you?"

What Uncle A.J. called a "mess," Father called "noise," which he thought would soon die down. Only a few days earlier, he had been talking about his hopes for my brothers' return: "Behzad will come back a doctor, Javid a computer programmer, and Albert the only architect I'll allow to add three new floors to number three Alley of the Distinguished——three for the three beautiful brides who will move in!"

But "the noise" had only escalated. And that night, Father was distressed, and to his misery Uncle A.J. added with every word: "My house is worth half what it was this time last year. These looters won't stop at the monarchists. They'll rob us all. A Jew who doesn't sell now, doesn't pack and run, is not just insane; he's an insane asylum."

Then he turned his attention to chewing his last bite. "Chew everything till it slips down like water," was one of the many sayings Uncle A.J. dispensed at every meal.

Father was silent. Born the last of six babies, none of whom had survived past their first few hours of birth, he was named Haghnazar, "Eyed by God," when he had lived for a full week. By then his doting mother told everyone that she had seen God in a dream, and how fortuitous! In it, He ordered her not to circumcise the baby until his seventh birthday, but to pierce his right ear and pass a hoop through it so he would never forget who had saved his life and to whom he must remain eternally a slave. So came about the hoop in the right ear of the impeccably dressed, middle-aged headmaster to some of the most notorious teenage boys of Tehran. Raised in Khonsar, a small village far away from Tehran, Father became the kid who made good: went to the big city, put himself through college, returned to the village, wearing the first suit the locals had ever seen, served in the army, left it after two years a decorated lieutenant, got a respectable job, married a city girl, and bought a house in the heart of the capital. To expect Father to sell the house, or go any farther than he already had—America or the moon sounded the same to him—was to undo the legend he had already become in the old village.

I could not see Father in the light of his past then. When he pondered an idea for too long, I believed my uncles, who secretly called him a wimp. He was missing the beat of opportunity, or so it seemed to everyone. I understood his refusal to become Uncle A.J.'s business partner. But why was the poet, the dervish, resisting the muse on the streets? Why was he hesitating to join the demonstrators? As I listened to the conversations around the table, my mind left only "wimp" unedited, while it corrected every other word: "looters" became "revolutionaries," "robbery" became "swift delivery of fairness." The masses were distributing the wealth among the deserved. I thought, Let the riches of north Tehran trickle south for a change. Chaos was how good things could be shared among people. And stealing from the rich was the only way to hasten the equality Bibi said the revolution would bring.

What did I understand of the revolution? Nothing I could put into words. But I recognized it when I saw it. It was in the air. And I breathed it. It was in every new sound, and every old sound that had died. Within weeks, Tehran seemed to have matured by years. Even drunkards stopped ranting about their personal misery. Neighbors did not fight. Cars honked constantly, but not in grid-lock, only to announce the advance of the uprising, or the fall of another barracks. Helicopters whirred incessantly. Vendors did not sing. With every footstep came the sound of glass breaking into smithereens. Mothers pleaded with their grown children. "Don't go!" pleas bounced off alley walls. In the daytime, marchers flooded the squares. In the evenings, martial law silenced their morning choruses. In the night we heard solitary shouts of "Down with the shah!" Every chant was followed by the shrill hoot of a soldier's whistle, a lengthy *Ist!,* Persian for Stop!, once, twice, and if a third time, it was followed by the pop of a gunshot, far away. If the shot was fired nearby, it sounded like a beam of steel falling. Still in denial, Mother insisted that it was the sound of a new construction just getting under way. In a way, she was right.

Even the city's trash changed. Suspicious ashes swirled in the air. Rocks were strewn on the pavements. Stray tires flared in the middle of every block. Half-burnt pictures of the royal family lit-tered the streets. Turned-over cars on fire, no longer an oddity, did not draw spectators. Canals carried the debris of the city's gallantry: pamphlets, bloody socks, torn sleeves. The marble pedestals in squares shed their statues. Teenagers mixed the city's new favorite cocktail—Molotov—and served it through the windows of banks and liquor stores. Demonstrating children walked up to soldiers and put carnations in the barrels of their rifles. With every flower, a little loyalty perished among the ranks of the royal army.

The makeup on the faces of women turned pale. Subtle was in. The fashion in youth footwear was sandy- or mauve-colored "kickers" half-boots. Despite their steep cost, they exuded the highly popular populist look. Denim had never made a bigger statement, particularly if paired with tartan-patterned, two-pocketed shirts. Khaki was the new black. Black, the shade of grief, was rarely worn, for a color so potent had to be used sparingly. White meant anything but peace. White burial shrouds were put on by men, who stood before armored tanks with empty hands. And red, the color of blood, was worshiped more ardently than ever. Red streaked from the handprints on the walls, sometimes captioned "This is the blood of martyr!" in case the sanctity of the shade was lost on someone unfamiliar with our primordial vogue. Any hint of red on the ground brought groups of men together, who gathered around, mournful but energized, as my uncles had around the slain sheep in Grandmother's courtyard.

On the way back from Grandmother's home that night, Mother and Father talked about A. J.'s advice. Mother believed Father had to heed it and sell our house. Then their conversation became an argument. Her voice rose, and her posture spitefully turned the way the posture of arguing couples turn in a car: one hypnotically fixed on the road, the other on the passenger window—wistful for the passing opportunities. For the first time in my life I was seeing my parents fight and wondered whether I had been too young to recognize their fights before, or whether they had never fought. Perhaps my adoring brothers had shielded me from the dark side of our family. Whatever the reason, there I was in the backseat as Father sped down the road, trying to beat the curfew, while Mother called him a man who could not guide his family in a prosperous direction. Drowning Mother's voice in his own, he repeated, "Woman! *Hatati veti pashati!*" Though I never understood what those words meant, they sounded frightening. Something about the way he clenched his jaw, steamed and hissed the *t*'s, the *v,* and the *p* through his teeth, made him resemble a pressure cooker on the verge of bursting.

I wanted nothing more than to be on the streets walking barefoot, alone. Soon their escalating voices became a joint cry, a single text of acrimony, sounding more muffled to my drifting awareness as it got louder:

"Oh, your fancy brothers! . . . *They are realists!* . . . Sell! Poof! Like that. Like it's a shoe . . . *Dale Carnegie says, Taking risks and sound advice is the key to success* . . . Taking advice from the village idiot is lunacy . . . *Village? Village! Village is what you never left* . . . Be sensible! . . . *Be daring!* . . . Be quiet! . . . *Be a man!* . . . *Hatati veti pashati!* Woman! . . . *Think America, our children* . . . Sure, we'll have Shabbat dinners at Jimmy Carter's . . . *We'll make friends* . . . Speaking sign language like the deaf and dumb? . . . *We'll learn* . . . We're old . . . *My other suitor* . . . Uh, uh, uh, don't go there, Helen . . . *I'll* . . . You'd never . . . *I?* I . . . You, you . . . ou . . . ouu . . .oution! Revolution!"

That night in the car, like the two halves of my family, I split and jettisoned the happier half of myself over the wobbling heads of my parents and watched it leap weightlessly onto the sidewalk. Not to those screaming strangers in the car, but to the streets, to their rapturous cascade that beckoned me with undeniable clarity, I belonged. To the revolution I belonged. To the rage that unlike me had broken free. It would guide me as no one else could, raise me as no one else knew how. And to be its daughter, I would emulate it in any way I could.

The following night in the synagogue, I sat in the children's section behind David Rohani. He was an eighth-grader who led every hymn the congregation sang. In all of my twelve years, I had never known a bigger celebrity. He ruled the congregation. Our surly cantor flashed his only smiles at David, whenever he came upon a hymn. That was David's cue to rise. Two hundred congregants held their breath and did not lift a foot lest their chairs creak, waiting for him to sing the first line. And when he had, the hall burst. David was not God. But with golden hair and green eyes, he had to be high in the heavenly ranks, which was where everyone insisted his voice came from.

Sitting under the main chandelier, dipped in its incandescence, I was so close to him that I could hear his fingers play in anticipation with the corner of the pages of his prayer book. For weeks I had watched him and tried to mimic his mannerisms. I was onto his tapping foot, the illicit metronome he kept under his chair. I even knew when he would inhale hard by watching how far his rib cage inflated to fill the folds of his white shirt. At home I would go to the rooftop, stand on top of the outhouse, wherever I could be alone, to practice singing like him. Within weeks I had memorized all weekly and special holiday hymns. David was to graduate that year. His exalted spot would be empty. He needed an heir. And there was a "dream" candidate to fill in his shoes.

After the services, I approached Mr. Modara, the head of the youth programs at the synagogue, and asked if he had a minute. He grinned and with it the tiny kinked hairs that peeked out of his nostrils parted. "I always have time for my girls," he replied.

To keep my most serious face on, I knew I had to avert my eyes from his nose and his ears, where a few more hairs curled out. Fixing my gaze on his mouth, I reminded him of my perfect attendance record. He nodded and said that of the great Mr. Hakakian he expected nothing else. Aiming for direct praise, I settled for the oblique.

I mustered all my courage but could only remind him of my Hebrew and Bible scores: a solid twenty on all oral and written exams. His smile still intact, he squinted to probe my face for what he sensed I was leaving unsaid. In the synagogue courtyard, surrounded by several congregants, Father was talking to his friends, oblivious to my predicament. The synagogue keeper was lurking at the door, waiting for the laggard to gather themselves. Among them was David's mother, reveling in the compliments another congregant was paying her son, each followed by a *"Mashallah!"* None of these faces helped me find the words I needed to begin, until Mr. Modara looked at his watch and warned, "I sure hope you'll talk before the curfew creeps up on us."

And I blurted: "I'd really like to, if I may, if it's possible . . . It'd be really, really stupendous if . . ."

I had resorted to Mother's advice to always be polite (the first item on all her shopping lists was "Greet the shopkeeper!") but found no way beyond politeness.

Rushing to my rescue, he gently said, "If what?"

"If I could sing the hymns."

"You're singing them, aren't you? I see your lips move."

"No, see, what I mean is, it'd really be stupendous . . ." I had hoped my carefully selected superlative could do everything that I was not able to. But the look on Mr. Modara's face told me that it had not. *Courage, Roya, courage:* "If I may, I would like to sing them like David Rohani."

"You should practice a lot to sing that well. His voice is angelic."

"Oh, I have. A lot. And I want to sing . . . I want to lead is really what I mean—after he graduates, of course."

His lips gathered. The bow of his smile darted upward and knotted his brow. "Are you saying that you want to replace David?"

"If I may, that'd really, really be . . . yes. I'd like that a lot."

"Well, Roya dear, you may not."

"Why not?"

"I can't explain."

"But I . . . . I don't understand . . ."

"I know you don't. But I can only tell you that you may not, and you should ask your parents why."

"But I—"

"No 'but.' I'm sorry, but the best reason I can offer is 'cleanliness.'"

"But I'm very clean. You can ask my mom. I shower every night before bed and I—"

"Roya, listen: it's not for me to tell you any more. Go talk to your mother."

I confided Mr. Modara's riddle not to Mother but to Farah. I poured my heart into the receiver the moment I heard her say "hello." At first, she chuckled, and I knew even without seeing her how she had tossed her hair back, as she did whenever she struck the pose of the wise elder, and threw her left eyebrow up until she spoke: "How many times must I tell you we are women?" Good heavens! Her pearls of wisdom were rolling my way. "You don't get it. We're women and this is our lot. Have I not told you this a thousand times?"

Could she just tell me what cleanliness meant? I begged, growing more exasperated by her mysterious allusions. She talked cryptically of blood and its imminent flow out of my body—where, when, why, or how, she would not explain until she saw me at Grandmother's the next day. All I needed to know was that it had already defiled me. Defiled! What did a word so unkind have to do with me? I hung up the phone even more puzzled. Blood, the blood that flowing out of a sheep's body was so holy, was unclean flowing out of my body? Why? What made one clean and the other . . . bad? Was it "bad" she had in mind, but called it "filthy" on the telephone? Filthy? Me? I had seen a protester, clubbed in the face, be raised upon the arms of men, his bloodied shirt instantly a talisman. I had seen the group of mourners, their heads wrapped in white bandannas, slap their chests, stand in a circle, and with chains flagellate themselves, with daggers beat their heads until blood gushed forth. No matter how young or old, that bleeding head was venerated. And not my blood?

The next morning passed more slowly than the week that had led to it. I snuck into the shower and filled the tub. In the drawers, I searched for Mother's bath potions. No one scrubbed with as much fervor as Mother. No one knew better than she the very address of cleanliness: the corner of Damascus Street and Pahlavi Avenue, where she and I took baths until a shower was finally installed in our home. In the vicinity of that bathhouse, every cheek turned rosy, every head glistened, every palm wrinkled. Its pristine walls and floors were spotless: NO STREET SHOES ALLOWED! RUBBER SLIP-PERS AVAILABLE IN ALL SIZES. And at its entrance, the arsenal of cleanliness, Mother's favorite line, was on sale: in transparent plastic kegs with black screw tops, golden Glemo shampoo; rows of Palmolive soaps; a pyramid of pumice stones; an assortment of *kisseh,* the industrial-strength human Brillo mittens that did all but lacerate the skin; diamond-shaped loofah made of the vegetative derivative of barbed wire; rows of Nasset razors; packs of Vajebi shaving cream, so potent a formula it contained traces of arsenic; and Rooshoor, the ivory cleaning bonbons drawn like chalk at the touch of which skin confessed every last bit of impurity.

Upon our arrival, Mother and I were assigned a number that marked our private quarters. A tiled room with a shower and a pedestal engulfed us for no less than three hours, during which Mother first started by scrubbing me and quit only when I had nothing but capillaries left to slough. If we arrived too late in the afternoon, after the second hour, the bathhouse manager, too familiar with Mother's lengthy stays, hurried us by flicking the lights. After three flicks, Mother shouted, "Dry!" and towels appeared on the bench in the vestibule where we dressed. On the way home, I was the weary hero returning from a long but victorious war.

In our own bath at home, I felt my time had come. It was my turn to do what I had watched Bibi, with sensuousness, and Mother, with seriousness, do in the shower. It was time for me to show that I, too, had learned the ways of adulthood, the ways of womanhood. I waded into the water, soaked, brushed, scrubbed, even shaved my hairless legs, and emerged only when blotches of red grew on my skin. There was the proof! The blotches would convince Farah and perhaps even Mr. Modara, whom I had plans to revisit soon. So red was my skin that afternoon, I had no choice but to cover myself by wearing a turtleneck, and a pair of panty hose under my clothes. While my hair was still damp and tame, I parted it and put a pin on either side. When Mother saw me, pleased that I had so eagerly readied myself for a visit to Grandmother, she called me luminous.

As my parents got ready, I lay on the living room floor to watch television. Suddenly I saw an image where there used to be no reception. It was the close-up of the mullah: A black turban. A broad forehead. Two dark, bushy eyebrows, not simply trailing off but arching sharply at the ends. An amorphous beard, gray and distinct by the way it was embedded in blackness, like a stray cloud in a night sky. Sky! . . . Ah, this was the profile Bibi had traced for her mother in the moon. This was Agha. The same sharp nose. The same stern face. When the camera pulled back, his profile was framed in the small panes of an airplane's window. This was the savior on a plane returning to Iran, just as Bibi said the great Hafez had predicted: the devil will flee, the angel will arrive.

My heart began to race. Not in the moon or on a wall, this was Agha in the flesh. If Father was watching, he would call him a "stinking mullah." Mother would ask what the *gezerah* was barking today. Another word by instinct I knew to mean diabolical. Was he? Or was he the angel? Who was telling the truth? Javid's words rang in my ear: "You must always think. If you do nothing else in life, remember this: Think!" I stared at the screen and looked carefully, but except for the contrast of Agha's dark cloak against the white panels, I saw no more. He was motionless, expressionless. He turned his head and the camera caught his eyes for a moment, but quickly he averted them. He assumed his profile once again and stared into the stowed serving tray of the seat ahead, as if he was looking into an abyss.

An English-speaking voice in the background asked a question. The frame widened to reveal the cabin and the other passengers. A clean-shaven man brought his face to Agha's ear and translated the words: "He is asking how you feel." The profile remained unmoved, eyes still gazing at the seat ahead, lips stretched to a smirk but no farther. Agha retorted, "How I feel? . . . Nothing!" The man translated "nothing" for the reporter, holding the microphone. The reporter, confirming the answer, repeated, "Nothing?" The assistant asked Agha again. The reply was the same. The profile was the same. And the abyss, just as vast.

Nothing! The angel Bibi had so richly described was feeling nothing. Nothing was the second one-word answer I had heard from an adult that week. What a pair it made with "cleanliness." Neither made sense. The first had puzzled and the second disappointed me. Any other answer—"unhappy," "confused," "worried," "sad," "uncertain," even "don't know at the moment"—would have been far better than "nothing." And not just any "nothing." Not one delivered with jitteriness of being overwhelmed. An irreverent "nothing" told with an unmistakable smirk. *Think, Roya, think.* "Nothing" must be a clue, like all the other clues. Like the little black fish, the dagger, and the pelican. "Nothing" could be another symbol or metaphor, like the devil or the angel. But I could not find meaning in so severe an expression, so sterile a word.

The next image was of Agha standing next to a uniformed airline steward at the top of the portable ramp of an Air France plane. With his right hand, the steward held the railing; he offered his left hand to Agha. Grabbing the steward's gold-embroidered cuff, Agha held the two corners of his robe in his other hand and took his first step. At each step, he paused and looked carefully under his feet. His legs moved slowly, heavily—truly like a man returning from the moon. Two, three, four, five. He descended and quickly vanished among the expectant crowd. Nothing could be seen of him but his turban bobbing among army caps. There was a frenzy of incoherent sounds. Cameras clicked. Voices mixed in a staccato of orders and prayers: "To the left." "No, to the right." *"Allahu-Akbar."* "Stop here." "Move, move, move!" "Say '*Ya Ali!*'" "His Holy Eminence's arrived." "Mister, out of the way!" *"Allah-o-ma-sal-e-ala-Muhammad-va-al-e Muhammad."* The caps circled around the turban. The turban bobbed and inched forward. The frenzy continued. Outside, the street looked the same as the sidewalk. The sidewalk the same as the square. Red light the same as green. Trees the same as the buildings, even those half-finished with exposed beams. Canals the same as the roads. Electric poles the same as monuments: all covered in humans. The ground and the air to any heights that could be climbed had been. Only the sky was void of bodies.

Atop a van, two mullahs in brown robes, holding megaphones, ordered the crowd, "Please go home! If you love Agha, go home!" But the orders were ignored. The crowd did not budge. Then the camera shook and erratic images flashed on the screen. When the camera became steady again, a sea of humans appeared, and it rippled with men, women, old, and young. A motorcade arrived. Once the rows of motorcycles and security cars passed, a white pickup glided through. Its roof and hood were covered with bodies. It inched forward, as Agha had among the military caps. Its path had to be cleared of the euphoric bodies that kept flinging themselves in front of its tires. Had "nothing" reached their ears? The plea blared in the megaphones again: "If you love Agha, go home!" But to plead with that crowd was to reason with the hurricane. So rapt they seemed by the moment, howling, sobbing, beating their chests, throwing their fists in the air, they were deaf to any pleas, except those of their own nerves. If they heard anything, it was only "If you love Agha," and when they heard that, their fists flew higher, they wept harder, as they had during his speeches, and they beat their chests more to show they loved him. *You cry. You suffer. It is how loving is done.* Was this the love Jahan said Hafez meant, on the night his family came to visit? *He who commands so much, he for whom so many tears were being shed, reproves, passes over the corpse of his martyrs lightly as the wind.* Is this agony that love? Was he, was all poetry, preparing everyone for this moment?

The next image was of Agha sitting on a makeshift stage in front of a microphone in Tehran's cemetery with his surrounding millions milling on the graves. The audience shouted, "Salute to Khomeini! Salute to Khomeini!" And he, seated, waved his hand. It was a strange wave. His arm rose not above his head but stretched in front of his chest, moving from side to side, as if to object, as if to wave the crowd away. *No,* the arm said, and the chants became louder. *No, no,* the arm moved, *enough!* Standing above them, he began to tap his hand in the air, as if he were smacking everyone on the head. Then his voice, the contemptuous lullaby I knew, echoed:

"This Mohammad Reza Pahlavi, this vile traitor on the run, plundered everything. He destroyed our country and built our cemeteries instead. Destroyed our economy. His so-called reform brought us nothing but misery. He held our culture back. He, his government, his Majles are all illegal. I will appoint a government. I will whack his government across the mouth—"

Just as I was beginning to ponder the words, the sound was cut off. Within seconds, the image froze. Then the image disappeared altogether into snow. These interruptions in the routine operations of television conveyed to the viewers, better than the news broadcasts, that something strange had happened yet again.

I went into the courtyard to peek at the alley. But the alley had vanished behind the empty kerosene containers that dangled from the rope and a cordon of fuming customers. Only glimpses of it flashed when the line moved, the containers were pushed forward, and the bodies took a step forward. I kept the door ajar with one foot, leaned out as far as I could, and tried to scan the queue for the breaking news. A man in a long dark coat and a goatee separated himself from it and stood to one side. He was proposing that Crown Prince Square be renamed Samad Behrangi Square. The queue fell into disarray. Some seconded the new name, others turned their backs in protest. Suddenly I had a view of the foundation gates. Dressed in civilian clothes, the Corpulent Cop was nimbly pacing the gates, talking with Bibi. Z and her brothers each held the corners of a sandbag, then dragged it to where they were making a barricade. Great-Uncle watched them. The man with the goatee proposed to take a poll: "In the honor of democracy, let us see what the majority wants." Another jolt of excitement shimmied down the queue. Several people separated from it to help with the polling. And when they did, I finally had a view of the building across from our home. Next to the "Down with the shah" on the wall, a new graffiti appeared: "Johouds Get Lost!"

In the *Mo'in's Persian Dictionary, Johoud* is: 1. a Jew; 2. the yellow piece of cloth Jews sewed on their garments to distinguish themselves; 3. an assiduous person; 4. fatty intestinal refuse. But in the Hakakian lexicon, *Johoud* had only one meaning: a world, a word that Father buried before he left the village. There *Johoud* meant "dirty." Throughout Father's childhood, *Johoud* was a word that mushroomed in the mouths of his classmates on rainy days. On those days, he was told to stay home, lest a splash off his body sully a Muslim classmate. But Father would never admit to having run into anti-Semitism. Holding his mother's hand, he only admitted to having met certain "bad people." *Johoud* was what she obliterated from the school vocabulary. Once, when the rain had not stopped for four days, she went to meet the district superintendent of the Greater Khonsar and begged to let her son attend school. Moved by her ardor, the superintendent stormed into Father's classroom, interrupted the lesson, and demanded that someone fetch him a glass of water. The class representative obliged. Then the superintendent handed the glass to Father and ordered him to drink a sip. Eager to please, Father took a huge gulp. Then the superintendent grabbed the glass, drank the rest, slammed the empty glass on the bench, and roared, "If that water was good enough for me, it's good enough for all of you. From now on, Haghnazar will be in class every day, in all kinds of weather."

"With that glass of water," Father triumphantly ended this particular anecdote, like a curator recounting an ancient time for an oblivious generation, "that decent man washed *Johoud,* shmohoud, and all that nonsense down for good!"

Forty years later, there was *Johoud* again on the wall across from our door. It was punctuated by a strange sign. Not one I had ever seen: a plus sign gone awry, a dark reptile with four hungry claws. I ran inside to tell Father what I had seen. He followed me to the courtyard and peered over the crowd at the wall. When he turned ashen, I knew he had seen the words. The pollsters on the queue became aware of him. They traced the gaze on his pallid face to the words on the wall. He turned away, pulled me to him, and shut the door while whispering, "Inside, Roya, inside." I asked what the sign was. He said with a broken voice, "Something from the Nazi days. Nothing you need to know. No good."

Inside, the news was no better. The phone rang. It was Aunt Zarrin. Guessing what she was telling Mother was easy by listening to the rise and fall in Mother's tone. First a sigh of relief, which meant Farah was fine! Then a cry of joy! And a "Thank God!" Farah had given birth. And the next natural question: *What is the baby?* Then the plummet in mother's pitch was enough to know what the baby was. An "Oh!" said with the joy fading from her voice. Then a blessing: "May you make her a bride!" The baby was barely an hour old.

Mother put the phone down and asked Father and me to go to the hospital. Father said no. Just no. Mother insisted. Father repeated his austere answer. But Mother worried that without the family at her side, Farah would be traumatized. We had to go at once, she repeated. His eyes fixed on the television, his complexion still pale, Father said, "Just go see what's behind our door."

Minutes later, Mother returned, slapping her hands, her face, even her thighs. With every blow, she hurled her grief at herself, and with every word, at Father: "What sane person would ever buy a home from a Jewish family in such turmoil?" she kept repeating as she slapped herself. A lifetime of sweating and saving, up in smoke! She shook from side to side, just as Grandmother did when she was in shock. Instead of sitting, Father was squatting on the living room rug, staring into the television. He said nothing while Mother reeled: "Had you listened to A.J. or me and put the house on the market . . ." None of her sentences had an ending. Mother did not end her sentences, because at bitterness she was the better poet, more sparing with words than Father. His lips parted. The lines on his forehead deepened. He appeared wan, fizzled down to only a shell of himself. Mother called his name: "Mr. Hakakian!" No reply. In one breath, she insisted that we leave for the hospital; in another, she warned that it was unwise to leave. From the dead end of her logic, the only exit led to Father: his resignation, lack of leadership, just at the moments when everyone needed him, like Farah in the hospital and my brothers in America. It was time that he rose up and quit being a "namby-pamby."

And rise he did.

At the crack of Mother's last words, Father's silent shell broke apart. An unfamiliar man emerged and stood on two feet. Stepping on the marble slab of the windowsill, he pulled the blind and opened the window. Then he perched on the sill and heaved himself into the courtyard. Under the junipers, he began whirling.

He whirled and raved. Raved and whirled. With fading balance, he unbuttoned his shirt. Then he raved, whirled, and swung the shirt in the air. It draped the fountain spout. Even dizzier, he lurched forward, took off his undershirt, swung it, and let go. It landed on the rosebush. His torso bare, he raved and staggered. Dumbstruck, Mother and I watched. He slowed, hunched, and undid his belt. His pants dropped to his feet. The pants around his ankles, he ranted and falteringly whirled on, till he stumbled, and took them off. Another swing. They caught on the branches of the wintersweet. No longer was Father a man but a spindle, spun by madness, spinning madness into yarns of madness. He reached for his waist once more. And then something else happened. This time, in me. Were it not to sear in my chest, I would have called it sadness. But it did. And I did not know its name. I ran away from the window, out of the living room, away from Father, the alley, its walls, and the queue—to the only place I could run.

The thick tar surface of the rooftop cushioned my feet, the token tenderness of that afternoon. I walked to the edge, the ledge pressing at my knees. The courtyard looked forlorn. The only life in the dry pool, the only blooms on the boughs, were clothes. Dwarfed by shame or winter, the junipers looked no taller than the plane trees alongside the alley. Everything was suddenly unrecognizable: my parents, the courtyard, the neighborhood, even my own body as I wrapped my arms around my chest and felt it hurt even at my own touch.

In the alley, the crowd huddled around the man with the goatee. They could not reach a consensus. More flammable than the oil they were waiting to buy, each customer roamed the alley ready for another debate, for a new slogan to chant, for a world to fight. They stood with command, as if the alley was where they dreamed to be; waited patiently, as if waiting was their destiny. Every few minutes, their voices rose: "Yankee, go home!" "May the shah go blind, our winter is as mild as spring." All of them were confident that God was on their soaring side.

Father had gone inside, but I could hear him shouting at Mother. His voice wove into the sounds coming from the alley. The rooftop was my only refuge in an impenetrable universe—a beguiling universe all around, beckoning, calling to everyone but me. Then came a revelation: Why not give it a call of my own? A howl of my own? Why live? What the alley wanted was not a great mind but a great daring of anyone willing to die. An occasion to which even *I* could rise. The revolution's design for the future was not so clear. But its demand for sacrifice was certain. The demonstrators knew how to die. So did I. Unlike everything else, death did not puzzle me. I had been prepared for it. I had seen a sheep leap to its death, and I could fly to mine. What better place than the grounds of our beloved courtyard, in whose grooves the memories of our happy days were embedded? What more peaceful a place than under the shade of the junipers? What better time than now? While everything seethed to the surface, a fog rising to the sky, I would dive into the earth. I, too, would leave my own mark of blood—become a hero.

I opened my notebook. Writing had always been a way of arranging words into beautiful metaphors on the page. But sitting in that corner, the prickly ledge needling my skin, I could not think of a metaphor. It was cold. Tears stung my cheeks. My bottom on the hard ground was going numb. Ugliness was everywhere. Yet I had to write. I pressed the pen between my fingers and began:

"Dear brothers!" But soon after I wrote those words, I crossed them out. They had abandoned me. They deserved no mention.

I began a new line: "Dear notebook!" A proper start! Let them know that at my loneliest, I had only a pen and a notebook at my side. Let Father know that I held a pen in my hand but found no way out: "These are the last words I will ever write because today I am going to throw myself off the roof. . . ."

The words flooded the page, a detailed report of everything I had seen. I wrote fast and gripped the pen hard, so hard that the left side of my middle finger paled and began to buzz. Several pages later, I still had more to say. An hour went by. Maybe two. Exhaustion set in. To do the note justice, I needed a break. I rested my head against the notebook, over the ledge. Soon my eyelids drew together and I fell asleep. When I awoke, I read what I had written. Then I read it aloud. The bitter allure of the words was intoxicating. It had a hint of the allure of the revolution. Its immensity had a force I had never felt within. Nothing chaotic or desperate. Uproarious, but rhythmic, too. Even songlike. A song not unlike the hymns I had heard in the synagogue, yet more moving, for I alone was its singer. To sing it, I needed no permission, no one's seal of cleanliness. At last, a place where I was welcome! There on the rooftop, pen in hand, I led my own chorus of words, with a melody of my own making.

Suddenly, between the covers of my notebook, a world had come into being. I read on and on. And when I tired of reading, I wrote some more and just kept on writing.

And I kept on writing.

7

FRESH AIR, SINGING DOVES, BUDDING FLOWERS, SASHAYING SPRING, AND OTHER POSTREVOLUTIONARY MIRACLES

ALL MITRA WAS TRYING TO SAY WAS "WHAT A SERENE DAY the sky predicts!" but standing in front of the class in a semicircle of our fellow eighth-graders tormented her. She had to rest her book on the teacher's desk because her hands, jittery with nervousness, could not hold it steady. One line was enough to tie Mitra's tongue. One line was all it took to choke every bit of confidence in her. An eternity passed and Mitra was still stuck on the third word: "W-w-w-w-w-hat, s-s-s-s-s-s-s-s . . . Sorry. Sorry, missus," she pleaded with our teacher, Mrs. Ebrahimi. "Please. I'll do it over. W-w-what, se-se-se serene day . . ."

She suffered reading. We suffered listening. A year ago we would have groaned. But this was 1979. April 1979. The revolution had been triumphant. And the nation was ecstatic. The sigh, the groan, the petulance, the merest hint of dissatisfaction, had flown out of Iran with the shah. Negative sentiments were nowhere to be found within our borders, nor snobbery in our schools. Victory had brought every citizen infinite patience. No parent ever wants a child to stutter. But if stuttering was what a child had to do, 1979 was the perfect year for it. It was also the perfect year for a child to show up for class with missing buttons, grubby fingernails, a stale lunch, and a low IQ. Ships carrying the poor, the tired, the huddled masses, were sailing to the wrong shores. Iran was vying to be the Ellis Island of the world. A full 98.2 percent of Iranians had marked the "Yes" box next to "Islamic Republic" for their choice of government in a referendum, and now stood as one proud, righteous nation, crowned with benevolence, with the torch of hope in hand. And in their other hand there was a tablet; its inscription, not yet legible, is a sore matter best left for another chapter.

That day in literature class we were studying a play titled *The Tale of William Tell,* the story of a brave Swiss archer fighting against the occupying Austrian army. Passing Tell on the street, Governor Gessler, the lead antagonist, had been enraged by Tell's refusal to take off his hat and bow before him. He allowed Tell to choose his punishment: be killed, or shoot an apple off his son's head. These were the kinds of stories we read in 1979: historic accounts of chivalry, of confronting the opulent evil with empty hands. Fiction did not interest us very much that year, for our own reality had surpassed the wildest possibilities of any imagination.

Mrs. Ebrahimi was looking for volunteers to read the parts of the characters in the play. She stood in the aisle between the two rows of benches. I raised my hand, but Mrs. Ebrahimi looked past it: "We don't need a play to bring you out of your shell, Roya. We know how well you read. I'd like to give one of your quieter classmates the chance." I could hardly be disappointed. If 1979 was the year of the Mitras, the inarticulate, it was also the year of the Royas, the eloquent who serenaded them. And at my new school, I was already one of the top students. A new school yet again. Number three Alley of the Distinguished had been sold almost overnight to the only family willing to buy it, at a fraction of its worth. Father, Mother, and I had moved into a two-bedroom apartment in a new neighborhood. The past year, at my old school, where I was the only child going home at midday, had turned me into an outcast. Now I was making a fresh start. I was carefully charting my way among my new classmates. But among my teachers, I had already become the irreproachable bee of all bees.

So Mrs. Ebrahimi sweetly rejected me. Each part went to someone else—narrator, the Austrian knight, the shepherd, the fisherman, the wife of Tell, Gessler's right hand, the princess of the house of Hapsburg, down to the last peasant and foot soldier—and I raised my hand for every one. Mrs. Ebrahimi believed that the play was about the power of human tenacity. And there I was, her diligent pupil turning into the tenacious human she was teaching us to be. And though, unlike Tell, my tenacity was not rewarded, as the class chuckled each time my hand shot up, I was pleased with my share of laughs.

Those of us without a part sat in the back, while the lucky actors shuffled to the front. In the glow of the white fluorescent lights, the cast looked pallid. The blue walls, the sleeveless gray uniforms with navy shirts and jeans underneath, gave everyone a sorry hue. They all were shaking nervously, but Mitra was the most pitiful. Too many looks were fixed on her mouth. And feeling the weight of everyone's gaze, she blurted her lines long before her cue:

"Father, why did we not bow and salute the—"

"Because Ge-ge-ge-ge-ge-Gessler deserves no re-re-re-re-respect!"

Sensing our restlessness, Mitra entreated Mrs. Ebrahimi once more: "Missus, can Roya read in my place, please?" A hand at the edge of my eyebrow, I clicked my heels, ready to serve.

But our teacher stood her ground: "If you sit, I'll enter a zero for your reading grade."

Mrs. Ebrahimi had not budged, and we were delighted. Everyone was rooting for Mitra. But the more she read, the more bored we grew. I began leafing through the play and soon found a line, a part so small that it had slipped Mrs. Ebrahimi's attention. Six words spoken by "an elderly bystander" had remained unassigned. With this discovery, my friskiness returned. I began to follow Mitra attentively once again.

"You will pay for such unruliness, William Tell. No one has ever disobeyed the great Gessler and lived to tell about it. Guard! Come forth and place the apple on this unfortunate child's head."

Mitra had foamed at the mouth, and the grand finale was still ahead. She was in no shape to deliver another word, much less exude the spirit of patriotism. A few moments passed, while everyone noticed the approach of the unclaimed part. To a tired class, the line was yet another obstacle. All of Mrs. Ebrahimi's verve was gone now as she sat, her head steady on her fist, looking like she was daydreaming. The arrow flew from the bow. The story neared its climax. Tell had to prevail. His son had to live.

Such a long struggle for the archer, the oppressed Swiss, Mitra, our class, and Mrs. Ebrahimi, all for the sake of good. One valorous bystander had to register Tell's gallantry. Our teacher had to be reenergized. Mitra had to calm down and finish. This was 1979, when every day posed an opportunity for heroic transcendence. No call to patriotic duty had ever rung louder in my ears. I sprinted into the middle aisle and bellowed, "Great heavens! The apple has fallen!"

The class exploded. Mitra doubled over, both hands on her stomach, and laughed the fluid laugh of a valedictorian. Mrs. Ebrahimi, too, burst, threw her head back, and joy began to ripple along her throat. The few girls who were squatting now rolled on the floor. Chalk dust filled the air, as one of the girls flung herself against the blackboard and busted the chalk dust receptacle. In that hilarious haze, I stood, poised and gleeful, reveling in my cameo.

This was not Austria, and there were no archers among us, yet we all felt that we had witnessed a moment of glory. An apple had fallen in our time. And the nation was eager to register the details of what it had witnessed. Everyone was on a quest. Mrs. Ebrahimi's mission was to save the shyer of her girls, catapulting them to confident heights, if only for one hour and twenty-five minutes three mornings a week. She, too, had caught the pandemic of that year—the desire to lead. She wanted to lead us, not into a revolution, but into a show of boldness. A conservative Jewish woman in her late thirties, she wanted us to know that it was possible to earn a degree, wear starched shirts, knee-length skirts, and bright red lipstick, and make one's own money.

Even those who mourned the fall of the shah had been touched by the events of the previous several months. Everyone had gained a little more audacity and doubted the impossibility of what had once appeared unthinkable. Now the class the country revered was not the royalty, the celebrity, or even the clergy, but the "downtrodden." The imam had unearthed an Arabic synonym and anointed the poor with it: "All we have is because of these *mostaz'afeen*. We owe everything to these *mostaz'afeen*. We do everything for these *mostaz'afeen*." And in a school of several hundred middle-class Jewish girls, Mitra Mirakhor, the daughter of a blacksmith, *was* the *mostaz'afeen,* the embodiment of the exalted victim the nation would die to save.

Everything was changing. But I was not scared. At last life had clarity. For years I had sought and examined clues: a hanged fish, Javid's words urging me to think, Albert's departure, a dead writer, a tape recorder furtively played in a basement, had all led me to this moment. To the revolution. Finally the youngest Hakakian had a leg up. Albert was the genius; Javid, the popular one; Bez, the most congenial. But I, the dream, with eyes wide open, had seen what none of my siblings had. I had become the family's witness.

Our world was reinvented. The flag remained green, white, and red, but an Allah insignia replaced its old sword-bearing lion. Stamps were redesigned. The moments of chaos at the university gates, the oil queues, the "Down with the shah" graffiti, became the venerated images on them. New bills were printed. Portraits of bearded faces and turbaned heads took the place of the smiling faces and crowned heads. Censorship was abolished. Coco was free at last! Newspapers and magazines mushroomed. The calendar changed. On February 12 in 2537 (the year dating from the coronation of King Xerxes) we went to bed. When we woke up the next day, it was February 13 in 1357 (the year of the prophet Muhammad's migration from Mecca to Medina). Overnight, 1,180 years had fallen away—eons of daylight saved for posterity!

Regulations became superfluous. Cordiality guided everyone. Pedestrians yielded to moving vehicles. Moving vehicles treated the crowded stretches of the streets as if they were pedestrian crossings. Passersby hailed buses like taxis, and the buses stopped for them. Inside, most passengers hung on to the straps, and seats went empty. Elderly women, holding the corners of their veils under their arms, danced on the sidewalks or distributed sweets to strangers. At phone booths, people handed out two-rial telephone coins to others who needed to make a call. Every street or alley name received the prefix "former," to remind us that if history was changing, so was geography.

A new national anthem was composed. In the mornings, we lined up in the schoolyard and sang at the top of our lungs: "O Khomeini our imam / O Khomeini our imam / O you unceasing warrior / O you embodiment of dignity . . ." The lyrics made us laugh, but we sang anyway. Words did not matter in 1979. We sang because we were moved by a force that had elated us all. And feelings were all that mattered that year.

On February 14, two days after the victory of the revolution, began the romance that lasted a year. Nineteen seventy-nine was a year of love, though not the kind of love I had ever known: not the love between a man and a woman, a sister and a brother, a child and a parent; not love of art, work, or religion. It was the mother of all loves, so vast, so deep, that in it every other love could grow. Victory had been announced on television by the young anchor, who, along with eight hundred other workers at that network, had gone on strike the previous November. He appeared, slim and stunning in a black turtleneck, and proclaimed Iran no longer a monarchy. A short line spoken by the nation's heartthrob. Then his face, beaming a grin, faded into black. An image appeared: a cherry orchard, full of pink blossoms. Accompanying various shots of the trees were the notes of the single greatest hit song of that year. It was a poorly composed duet, played on a drum and a horn, and its lyrics remained on all our lips for months to come: "The air is fresh / The flowers are budding out of the soil / The returning doves are singing / Blood is boiling in the stem of every reed / The blessed spring is sashaying toward us . . ."

Even ordinary ads now read:

SALE! SALE! SALE!

HEREBY WE INFORM THE HEROIC PEOPLE OF TEHRAN
THAT IN CELEBRATING OUR HISTORIC VICTORY
"LE MAISON MISSUS YAMINI,"
HOME TO THE LARGEST SELECTION OF
WOMEN'S WINTER AND SUMMER CLOTHING, IS HAVING AN
UNPRECEDENTED SALE!

Darmoo Manufacturers (Mother was particularly happy to see this) printed a special announcement:

NOTICE!

TO FIGHT U.S. IMPERIALISM AND ALL OTHER EVILDOERS
DAROOGAR COMPANY VOWS TO PROVIDE
ALL ITS PRODUCTS AT THE SAME LOW
PRE-REVOLUTIONARY PRICE:

BAR OF PALMOLIVE SOAP: 13 RIALS
TRAVEL-SIZE PALMOLIVE SOAP: 6.50 RIALS
DARMOO SHAMPOO: 22 RIALS
CHILDREN'S SOAP: 14 RIALS

Next to the "Help Wanted" section of the dailies, row after row of congratulatory notes appeared:

THE WORKERS AND STAFF OF THE INDUSTRIAL AND
COMMERCIAL GROUP "NATIONAL" PROUDLY DECLARE THEIR
UNITY WITH THE VICTORIOUS REVOLUTION AND ITS
MAGNIFICENT, EXALTED LEADER, THE GRAND-AYATOLLAH
IMAM KHOMEINI AND HIS WISE, UNSELFISH PRIME
MINISTER, ENGINEER MEHDI BAZARGAN.

Though the ads varied slightly from day to day, the public kept on reading, dazzled by the multifarious signatories: the Stone-Cutters Union, the manufacturers of plumbing and aluminum by-products, workers of Hilton Hotel chains, the Center for Winter Sports, Cigarette Manufacturers of Iran, the workers of the Club Revolution (formerly known as the King of Kings Club), the workers of Prevention of Malaria and other Contagious Diseases of the Greater Zabol Region, the Seafood Producers of Southern Iran, the Syndicate of Liquid Gas Distributors, the Tailors Union, the Association of Traffic Meter Makers of Iran, the Staff of Saderat Bank, the Teachers Union of the First District . . .

It was time that we, the Teenage Jewish Girls of Raah-e Danesh Hebrew Day School, signed on to the revolution, too. It had not been our bloody handprints on the walls. The "Down with the shah" graffiti had not been in our handwriting. Nor had they been our mouths shouting *"Allahu-Akbar!"* on rooftops. But we were no less moved. And now we wanted to claim our share of revolutionary excitement. If we had lost our chance at making the revolution, at least we wanted to be among those who protected it.

We, too, wanted to deface the royal inscriptions from the stone entrances of bridges, paint a slogan on the wall, hoist an imam Khomeini frame onto a vacant pedestal, chant "Down with" or wish "Death to," since "long lives" were few and far between. Every day brought the warning of yet another threat posed by "bloodsucking American imperialism." Uncle Sam had the leading part of the enemy in the new era, with the shah, Menachem Begin, and Anwar Sadat, "Jimmy Carter's puppets," as the cast the nation had to shun. Did I say "nation"? That we no longer were. The imam referred to Iranians not as a "nation," but as the "faithful." And not simply *the* faithful, but the "ever-present-on-the-stage faithful," whose job it was to "whack the Great Satan America across the mouth" day and night. With each speech, he unveiled another reason for a massive protest. By "stage," he meant the streets, into which people flooded at all hours to protest. Ordinary citizens became an acting troupe whose industrious executive producer was the single largest nonpaying employer of all time.

Evil disguised itself in a thousand ways, but the imam spotted it every time. For the first few weeks after the revolution, it came in the guise of the shah's army generals, ministers, and associates. Every night, the proceedings of the summary trials that were held for them aired on television. There was no judge, jury, or defense attorneys. The former leaders had been stripped of their uniforms. Dressed in rags, they sat with hung heads wrapped in bandages. They looked horror-stricken. And of their storied titles and medals, all that remained was a cardboard sign of their names that dangled from their necks. They were asked not to speak but to itemize their acts of "disservice." Most were found guilty on charges of "sowing corruption on earth." And since justice could not be delayed, by dawn they were executed. No time was wasted, not even for the prisoner to prepare himself for his final hour. The executioners of the former prime minister Hoveida shot him in the back as they were ushering him to take his place before the firing squad.

Along with our cup of tea, we took in images of their corpses in the morning papers. With Kalashnikovs in their grips, young revolutionaries stood above the slain and smiled at the tableau they had painted: corpses of bare-chested middle-aged men on gurneys, their pants unzipped, mouths frozen in a last howl.

I smiled, too. I, too, believed those dead to be lesser people, if they were people at all. They had tortured the best minds of the country, put the feet of writers like Samad Behrangi in cement, and thrown them into rivers. They were nothing like me or us. They were beasts who had ravaged our land and caused the misery of the downtrodden. They had to be killed, for as the imam warned, "Left to their own devices, those 'humanoids' would fester and infect us again."

Among the executed bodies of the "humanoids" making the headlines one morning lay the corpse of Habib Elghanian, the wealthy Jewish philanthropist on whose donations all Hebrew schools had thrived. The details of his trial and execution were yet to be reported. But the foreboding reached our school far in advance. The footsteps of teachers in the hallways came without the murmur of conversation. Whispers swirled in the air instead. The courtesies they always exchanged as they passed through the corridors vanished: doors slammed shut without the insistence that the other pass first. The groundskeeper's broom echoed unaccompanied by the expletives he usually muttered.

As the hours passed, the rumors about the proceedings trickled in: The judges at the revolutionary tribunal had kept their backs to Elghanian, refusing to look a "Zionist spy" in the face. Anyway, how could they have faced a man with whose crimes the courtroom itself was reeking? The linoleum on the floor, the chairs on which they sat, the covers of the Koran on their tables, the tables themselves, the reading glasses they put on in order to write the charges against him, the pens themselves, all had to be entered as evidence. This spy was the most unbreakable of the unbreakables. Habib Elghanian was the founder of Plasco, the company that had brought plastic to Iran.

The charges against him sounded ancient, even biblical: "Friendship with the enemies of God, warring with God and His emissaries, and economic imperialism." The scene of the trial, the words that were exchanged, had invoked the memories of the old blood libels among the elder Jews. But those memories did not belong to my generation. My classmates and I remained loyal to the adolescent code of conduct and dismissed our parents' worries. Unfazed, we treated this particular corpse like all the others: one more enemy caught in his tracks.

The next morning had another unexpected event in store. This time the news was made at our school. Early in the day, an unfamiliar voice over the intercom summoned the entire student body to the lunchroom. A stranger on the makeshift stage was welcoming us. She was a woman wrapped in a black veil, pulled tightly from every corner, with only a small opening for her bright blue eyes. Short as she was, she appeared benignly nutlike: a solid black shell with a tiny chip to reveal her face. But when she began to speak, her colossal voice shockingly masculine, it became instantly clear that this particular nut was not the edible kind. Positioning herself under the framed image of Moses holding the tablets, she bellowed, *"Bism Allah al-Rahman al-Rahim.* Dear girls, daughters of the revolution, with salutations to our great imam and you. I am Mrs. Seyedeh Fatemeh Moghadam. But first, allow me to explain to you the significance of the Seyedeh in my title."

She took a piece of chalk, drew a vertical line on the blackboard, wrote two words on either side, and said, *"Seyed,* as in a man. *Seyedeh*—notice the 'eh'—as in a woman. Is it clear?" Striking her chalk on the word on the left, she enunciated: "Everyone repeat after me: Se. Yed. Man." Hopping to the other side, she tapped on the syllables of the second word: "Se. Ye. Deh. Woman. He or she, like myself, is a direct descendent of the prophet Mohammad himself."

Her cheeks inflamed, she turned to us once more: "And what must you say when you hear the name of the prophet? Ah, I can't hear it, girls." She tilted her head upward, pleading with the ceiling. Her eyelids fluttered, signaling something life-threateningly urgent as she gasped the phrases: "Come, uh, come now, where's, uh, uh, where is—"

Where, indeed! Where was our principal? Our assistant principal? What was a black-veiled creature doing strutting around our school? Her hand behind what would have been her ear were it not shrouded, she demanded even more loudly, "Give it to me! I'm here and will stay right here till I hear it!"

We stood quietly puzzled. Then she began pacing up and down the platform. Because of the cascading flow of her veil, her cake-walk had a beatific flair. Certainly she wanted to deliver a vital message. But she was too excited to do so. And being too stunned, we probably would not have heard it. Bouncing nimbly to the front of the platform once more, she leaned into us and hissed, "Whenever you hear the mention of the prophet's name, you must salute him and all his kin by saying the *salavat*. Now let us tryyy!"

The first time I had ever heard a *salavat* was from Z's great-uncle in her basement. It was a sound I always remembered with tenderness. But now this woman demanded that we repeat the words. A few voices meekly responded and that satisfied her: "Goood! Now that you know I'm the prophet's descendant, you ask, What's this woman doing here in our school? Well, as of today, I, Seyedeh Fatemeh Moghadam, will be your new principal. From now on, you'll be dealing with me and my assistant, Ms. Ghanizadeh." Her young assistant flashed a smile to reveal a comely dimple on each of her cheeks.

Mrs. Moghadam went on: "The two of us will be running your school. And we can't do our job without your participation. So when you go back to class, before resuming your regular activities, choose a representative among yourselves. Ghanizadeh and I will meet with each representative regularly to bring your school to the level of our revolutionary times. For now, that is all. You can go back to your classrooms."

The execution of Elghanian had not alarmed us, but Mrs. Moghadam's invasion did. Within days, the Jews of Tehran decided to take the most drastic measure of all: to visit the imam and to receive his personal guarantee that the community was as safe as ever in Iran. An ad hoc assembly, consisting of six men—two rabbis, one of them Father's best childhood friend, and four fiery young intellectuals—was selected for the job. The young among them had long dreamed of meeting Agha and believed in his message of equality for all. This was their revolution, too. As university students, they, too, had taken to the streets and demonstrated against the old regime. Agha had to learn that the Jews of Iran were not Zionists. Or, as they wished to clarify the term for him, they were not political Zionists. It was a distinction they had fashioned on their own, and what they really meant by it was that they saw no other homeland for themselves but Iran.

The rabbis, on the other hand, merely wished to plead with him to be good to the community, and to tell him of one of the lesser-known pillars of Judaism: True Jews are ones who share in the wishes of the society in which they live. And now that Iranian society wished to establish an Islamic republic, so did every good Jew.

The next day, before sunrise, the group piled into a station wagon and headed for Qom to meet with the imam. They vowed, no matter what transpired, not to leave Agha's home until they had heard words of assurance: a statement with which to hearten the community of their security under the new regime. Hours later, nearly at the threshold of the holy city, the pilgrims were beset by a trial. At the imam's quarters, one of the men suddenly remembered, they must all remove their shoes. And the fetid truth was that not all of them could do so without embarrassment. (At last, "cleanliness" caught up with even the holiest of men!) A sharp detour, a stop at a kiosk across the desert, and an eleventh-hour purchase of a fresh pack of tube socks were among the miracles of that blessed journey.

The men arrived late in the afternoon. They found the imam's residence empty of the usual throng of disciples. Soon they learned that the quiet was in honor of their visit. Waiting was unnecessary. Immediately after their shoes were off, they were guided into the pressroom. They had yet to seat themselves on the folded blanket around the edges of the rug at one end of the room, when the imam entered. Surprise threw the men into disarray. One of the rabbis rose to his feet. Following suit, the second rabbi also stood, leaving the others seated and befuddled. In his torpid manner, the imam insisted on remaining standing as long as his counterparts had not sat first. And they, following Iranian etiquette, refused to sit before a man of such stature.

When they had at last arranged themselves in a circle on the floor, the imam's aba swelled about him. His turban larger than usual, his neck buried under the beard, he was a holy bubble boiled up from the earth to receive the group. The young doctor, appointed to be the delegation's speaker, cleared his throat to begin. But one of the rabbis, clearing his throat on an even higher note, addressed the imam: *"Bism Allah al-Rahman al-Rahim."*

He invoked the name of God in Arabic, to show deference to the imam and to remind him of how assimilated the Iranian Jews were with Muslim tradition. Just like the hundreds of congratulatory ads in the newspapers, the rabbi congratulated the imam and expressed the community's joy in the new order. Every Persian speech always concludes with a poem, and so he ended his speech with a verse. In it, the prophets were likened to the sun and the moon, and the wise clergy to the brightest of the stars.

Then the imam spoke. His tone was stern, but his message, refreshingly balmy: "All three prophets were sent by God to guide mankind. All those heretical religions on earth never tended to the soul of mankind. But the three monotheistic religions do. They are the only religions to descend directly from heaven. They have an instruction about every aspect of human life. That is what they have in common. For instance, who a man should choose for a wife. How marriage must take place so that it results in a God-fearing offspring. How copulation must happen. What that mother must or must not eat during pregnancy. How she must live and conduct herself before and after the child is born. How she must nurse that child. And if she wishes not to nurse the child herself, what laws she must follow for hiring a nurse. And how often that child must be nursed and how the mother must and must not spend time with that child. And once the child is old enough to leave the mother's bosom, what guidelines must the father follow to educate that child."

The six men wondered how this speech related to the Jewish community, the execution of Habib Elghanian, or the takeover of a Hebrew school. If courtship, copulation, pregnancy, and delivery were symbolic of another meaning, it eluded them all. Yet they sat, waiting, listening.

"In the holy Koran, Moses—salutations upon him and all his kin—has been mentioned more than any other prophet. Prophet Moses was a mere shepherd when he stood up to the might of Pharaoh and destroyed him. Moses, the Speaker-to-Allah, represented Pharaoh's slaves, the *mostaz'afeen* of his time."

The moment the imam used the celebrated term to refer to the enslaved Israelites, the six men became confident that their long journey had not been in vain.

The imam ended his remarks by saying: "Moses would have nothing to do with these pharaohlike Zionists who run Israel.

And our Jews, the descendants of Moses, have nothing to do with them, either. We recognize our Jews as separate from those godless Zionists."

The shibboleth at last! *We recognize our Jews as separate from those godless Zionists! Imam Khomeini* was painted on the walls of every synagogue by nightfall.

The Jewish community had chosen its six representatives more swiftly than our class chose its single one. It would have been easy to decide who to send to Mrs. Moghadam if we had the faintest clue as to why she wanted to meet our representative "regularly." Classes had always had a representative. The chores of those representatives were small and obvious: getting chalk, reporting to the teacher who was absent and why. Besides, a representative was only accountable to the teacher, not the principal. Now Mrs. Moghadam wanted someone to meet her. Alone! In her office. And in the morning, too, while class was in session. No representative had ever been given duties during lesson time.

This election was like no other. We needed someone gutsy to be alone with the new principal, whom we had already come to call "the Megaphone." Someone who could be quick on her feet, know when to give in, but when to speak up, too. We did not know the stakes, but we did feel that they were great. In an unusual hush, we sat around and stared at one another, as if we had just met and were considering the impressions we had made. At last Nazila broke the silence: "I say we choose Roya."

Ziba asked, "Which Roya?"

"The new Roya. She's quick as a whip. And she knows big words. I don't understand what she says half the time."

I was just beginning to revel in "whip" when the rest of that line lashed. Parnian said, "Yeah. If she only dishes to the Megaphone some of the things she dishes in class, she will make her dizzy in no time. Besides——"

I did not like the direction this conversation was going, so I interrupted: "Hey, hey! What does that mean?"

In her gentle way, Nazila intervened: "Let's face it: You never study, and you ace every exam. You write the best compositions, and you talk better than adults. You're a genius."

Nazila and I had bonded on the first day of school, when I settled myself into the bench behind her. Her auburn head exuded warmth. Her eyes were the only eyes I had ever seen twinkle with laughter. And her permutations, as she laughed, brought laughter to everyone else: she doubled over, like a rubber bottle that had been squeezed, in perfect silence for a few seconds, then she gave a long squeal as she inhaled and stood straight again. But now she terrified me. Her praise terrified me. The acceptance I had longed to have from my old schoolmates was being given to me by her. Yet with every phrase my heart sank a little lower in my chest. Why? What was it I wanted to hear? Not genius. Genius scared me. *Crack!* was the sound of genius to me. Genius snapped all good things in half. It subtracted a presence from a family, shuttled its bearer to a faraway place. Genius was a lonely person. Genius was my brother Albert. And I did not want his destiny. I did not want to be shipped to America like him. Anything, anything at all, was better than genius.

I got up. I walked to the coatrack, grabbed a jacket, threw it over my head, and buttoned it under my chin. Pausing to compose myself at the blackboard, I took a piece of chalk. Then I turned on my heels, and the jacket fanned around my head and its sleeves flapped in the air. Leaning into the class, I said, *"Bism Allah al-Rahman al-Rahim.* Girls, daughters of the revolution. Let me tell you about genius."

I drew a vertical line on the board and wrote on one side: "Ge. Ni. Us. As in a man. Ge. Ni. Useh. As in a woman."

My hand behind my ear, I said, "Girls, girls, girls, I cannot hear you. You must always say what, when I tell you what?" Doing my best to seem on the verge of a swoon, I stared at the ceiling, fluttered my eyelids, and bent my knees. "Tell it to me, girls! Tell it to me good and loud!"

Through Nazila's squeals, the twitter of a *salavat* came. Cured by the magic words, I resurrected myself again and, with great verve, began to scribble the many breakdowns of the word *genius*. With every letter I wrote, their snorts and cackles, the plush range of their laughter, stroked my back. At last one of their gasping voices managed to say, "This? You call this one a genius? She's a nut!"

And another completed the thought: "And one nut deserves another. Roya's my pick."

Still undulating to laughter, rising, arching their backs and dropping again, some begging for a break—"Can't breathe, stop! Gonna pee in my pants"—they applauded in approval. But I had just begun. Now I was searching for a new word, when someone squeaked, "Excuse me, Mrs. Moghadam, can you please break down the word *nut* for us?"

Bug-eyed, I leaped and stood on a bench, then growled: "Salutations upon the great imam and all his kin! *Nut* is too easy at such a historic juncture. Let us try something more difficult to hone our Islamic skills. Let us try *fenugreek.*"

Back at the board once more, I wrote the name but also drew the herb. No longer softly plush, the roar of their laughter filled the air. (Not even expert herbalists like Dr. Jazayeri knew of vitamin F, the many felicitous qualities I unearthed in fenugreek.) A hiccupping voice gathered enough breath to say, "She's the best clown we've ever had."

Clown! What relief! *Clown* was the praise I longed to hear. It delighted me as no other had. Everyone nodded while they slowly recovered from fenugreek. I threw the chalk over my shoulder, hung the jacket back on the rack, dusted off my uniform, and joined them. Foolishness had kneaded me into their tender mix. We were laughing together now: they, at their clown; I, at my feeling of contentment. Gone were my days as a misfit. Together we were a perfect fit. For the first time in all the years I had been a student, I felt relieved. The gates had swung open, and I flowed through, to where I most wanted to be: indistinctly among them. Within a few months, my lonesomeness had ended. Yet another of the revolution's many miracles.

The next morning, Mrs. Moghadam, sitting behind her desk in Islamic uniform—a matching silk scarf, long, loose-fitting overcoat, and pants—waved me into her office. Her azure outfit had wrapped almost as much of her as the veil had, but softly so. Or perhaps the softness was emanating from her azure eyes, brighter now that they were not clouded by her veil. When I entered, she was deliberately stirring her tea in a glass cup. On her desk, I saw a folder with my name on it. She lowered her head, gesturing that I sit beside her. Her gaze fixed at the glass, she asked, "Do you see how this sugar cube melts in the tea?"

"Yes, ma'am."

"To me this sugar cube is every corporeal desire lurking in a woman's heart, everything that separates us as the faithful and must be sacrificed for the good of our revolution."

She withdrew the teaspoon from the cup, tapped it at the edge of the cup, and continued, "Look at it! It's perfectly sweet now, but there's not a bit of sugar to be seen." She lifted the cup and drank the tea in one gulp. She dabbed her lips with the back of her hand and picked up my file. "I see you're a top student. Especially in Persian composition. Nineteen out of twenty from the likes of Ebrahimi is tough to get. What was your last composition about?"

"The revolution."

"What about the revolution?"

"How good it's been. How free we are now. I wrote about writers who died because they defied censorship."

"Defied . . . huh? I like how you talk. But do you also know that we must be more vigilant than ever? Those Pahlavis are still among us. That's what I want you to do: be the eyes and the ears of our revolution in the schoolyard and in the classroom."

What began as a conversation quickly became a sermon. She sank back in her chair and talked till the bell rang. Her last request was that I round up the class every afternoon and bring them to the lunchroom. Instead of English, she would give us a series of lessons on Islam. Banging her white fist on the desk, she yelled, "What we need more of is not the language of those duplicitous British or criminal Americans, but the wisdom of the Koran and our imam. We can do away with English." And for a moment, our shared grudge against English bridged our disparate worlds.

At last she dismissed me. I walked to the door while in my mind I began to compose the report I would give to class: "Relax! Megaphone: weird but harmless!" But before I had stepped out of her office, she called me back inside once more.

"Roya, wait! Since you're so bright and know so much about the Jewish tradition, tell me, why do Jewish fathers take it upon themselves to deflower their daughters?"

Just in time for me to revise that last headline I intended to announce in our class: "Megaphone is the devil. This is war!"

I was right about war. Only Mrs. Moghadam's war was not over territory but people. We, the students, were the conquest she was eyeing. Years later I learned that on the résumé of a religious careerist, nothing shines more brightly than mention of an army of converts. With each one of us turned Muslim, she saw herself a step closer to a seat in the Majles. The lunchroom was her battlefield. Every afternoon she charged at us. Every afternoon we retreated a little. In the classroom we huddled together behind closed doors with our teachers, who, unlike us, were terrified of Mrs. Moghadam and turned to us for consolation. Just as they were about to formulate a thought, Mrs. Moghadam's stern footsteps would echo in the hallway, and instantly their voices fizzled into whispers: "Shhh! She's coming!" There we saw, better than in any laboratory, how an action created an equal, but opposite, reaction. Her unannounced visits blotted out the motivation in them to go on. To them Mrs. Moghadam embodied a return to the old days of segregation for Jews in Iran.

To us, she was a tyrant. And thanks to Agha, we had seen tyrants defeated with a good rebellion. Besides, the revolution had turned over the political soil in Iran. Mrs. Moghadam was only one of the many odd creatures that had reared their heads. There were boys handing out the Communist Manifesto at every major intersection; Maoists who sold Chinese flags on the campus of Tehran University; girls who marched behind the American feminist Kate Millett along the former Pahlavi Avenue; the Spartacusans, who believed that we were a nation of slaves and did not know it ourselves; members of the "Tornado Party," who considered Albania the world's greatest democracy and, therefore, the best model for Iranians to emulate. Unlike our teachers, we saw the religious, the Mrs. Moghadams, as the exception to the bright promise of the revolutionary future. Our Iran was safe from zealots. Prime Minister Bazargan and his cabinet of Western-educated ministers had been appointed to stop the advance of such extremists.

For the first few days, Mrs. Moghadam only asked questions: Should religion be passed on by heredity or by conviction gained through independent study? A euphemism for "Should you or should you not follow your parents into Judaism?" When she had settled the matter of whether following our parents blindly into anything, especially faith, would be a betrayal of God and the revolution, she asked a second question: Why, in the holy Koran, did God speak of the prophet Moses as the Kalim-Allah, "the Speaker-to-God," but of the prophet Muhammad as the Khatam al-Anbya, "the Seal of All Prophets"? She could never temper herself. She rushed to answer her own questions: Moses was indeed a prophet to whom God spoke, but some time later Jews lost the path of God. Therefore, God had to send another prophet to round up the stray faithful. So Jesus Christ was sent to do the job. But lo and behold, the Christians, too, wandered off that path. And God had to intervene one last time. This time He sent the prophet Muhammad, who put the faithful on the right path, from which they have not strayed since. Therefore the title "the Seal of All Prophets."

But one speech, the one that to her great surprise proved to be her last, changed everything for all of us. It came on a Wednesday. The lunchroom air was bright by April and thick with the scent of baking matzo. We had been called yet again to hear her, this time even earlier than usual. But we were in no mood. Thursday would be the eve of Passover, and in our minds, vacation had already begun: eight full days at home with family, and no one to lecture us. After the holiday not much would remain of our strange school year. We would take our finals, and think of what to do about school for the following year.

She walked in, dressed in her best shimmering silk set. Unlike us, our devout diva was high spirited, and ready to speak with more fervor than ever. As it turned out, this was an opus long in the making:

"My dear sisters, daughters of our great revolution! It's now time for you to learn about the delicious topic of corporeal sin. Yes, my sisters. Young and innocent as you are in your pubescent splendor, you are also diabolical. Diabolical and no less. Duty compels me to warn you of the perniciousness you all possess. You do possess it and don't even know it. Abomination lurks beneath your innocence. Oh, how loathsome it is. How lethal. More murderous than the poisonous dagger with which the evil Ibn-Moljam stabbed the pure heart of Imam Ali. More baneful than the hatchet of the Satan himself. Oh, my sisters, I'll walk on hot coals, throw myself in the way of eternal whirlwinds, die, before I allow you to let loose, unknowing as you are, the evil, the apocalypse that only you could bring upon us.

"You're certainly wondering how on earth you're capable of

drowning everything in eternal darkness. You're asking your-selves, Of what apocalypse is our beloved principal speaking?

"Ah, but I tell you. I speak of the apocalypse of your hair. Yes, hhhair. Such a simple word. So seemingly dead and blameless. But, my dear girls, blameless it is not. It is constantly scheming to reveal itself, peeking out of the scarf, even from under the veil. It peeks not to reveal itself to me or you, or your peers in this room, but to a man. You heard me right. Your long, beautiful hair is the very snake that deceived Eve, who then deceived Adam. That vile reptile never stopped. Hundreds of years later, it still deceives. One glance at your hair, even at a strand of your hair, is enough to turn any man into an irredeemable wanton, into a uni-corn beast, with a unique intention, each of his heinous tissues in unanimity, its projectile moving in a unified direction: that of sin. Do you understand sin? It is of sin that I speak to you. The sin that no ablution can cleanse. Sin that cannot be expiated. For this sin there is no penance, no atonement. No amount of alms can repair its consequences. Once the beast unleashes itself upon your inno-cence, you're not a child of Allah anymore. You're a child of Satan, and appropriate to your kinship, you deserve to receive a hail of stones and nothing less.

"You ask yourself, How does our sister, our mother and adviser, Moghadam wish us to behave?

"But why tell you in my inadequate words when there is the great example of Fatemeh, salutations be upon her and all her family? On the eve of her death, she pleaded with her man, her leader and protector, Imam Ali, salutations upon him and all his kin. Well, yes. I was saying. On the eve of her death, that most demure of women, Fatemeh, writhing in pain, was riddled with worry. Far more than her own unbearable suffering, she was worried about the very sin I have been warning you against. She said to Imam Ali, salutations be upon him and all his kin, 'My death is imminent. But I beg of you to not wait and bury me at dawn.'

" 'Why not?' asked the beneficent Ali, the saint of all saints. 'Why not, my considerate bride?'

" 'Because,' coughed the dutiful Fatemeh through tears gushing from her shining eyes and the sputum welling in her holy chest, 'men will be attending my funeral, and I do not wish for them to lift my coffin, lest they feel the weight of my feminine body, be aroused, and thus be led to sin.'

"From this shining example, what do we conclude? You know the conclusion. By now you fully understand what evil I speak of. I shall spare you the obscene. But it is, I'm afraid, up to me to teach you how to avoid it. If a man walks into this hall at this very moment that I stand before you without my veil, what must we do? You look at me and say, 'Mrs. Moghadam is covered from head to toe. We cannot see a strand of her hair.' Even now that I have my scarf pulled to the edge of my eyebrows, and its trail covers all of my neck, even now that my long sleeves reach my knuckles, and my uniform touches my ankles, even now, my sisters, daughters of our glorious revolution, that my pants fall to the heel of my shoe and my shoes leave not a centimeter, not even a millimeter of skin exposed, even now I feel naked. Yes. You heard right. Naked, if a man were to walk in.

"In the West, in that superficial, artificial, morally corrupt country called America, where they know not of God, where they live by the rules of Satan, where they drink alcohol instead of water, consume an animal as filthy as a pig, and lead promiscuous lives, where women walk naked in the streets, fornicate in public, and conduct orgies in their homes—there, the headmasters train their students for insignificant trials, for an emergency such as fire. They conduct fire drills in their schools. But we! We, my sisters, daughters of our great revolution, we're not afraid of earthly threats. We fear only one fire: the eternal fire of hell.

"So the drill that I'm preparing you for is a 'man drill.' Learn this and you have bought yourselves a one-way ticket out of hell. If a man were to walk into this room, I, naked as I feel without my veil, would have no choice but to pull the hem of my Islamic uniform over my head. And you say to yourselves: But Mrs. Moghadam would be exposing her body. But at that moment of emergency, when I have not even a second to lose, I must cover my head better than any other part. So, girls, if I scream, 'Man! Man! Man!' what must you do? Run if you can. And if you can't, hide. And if you can't hide, surrender, and pull the hem of your uniforms over your heads.

"Just so you never forget, I'll demonstrate: tug at my scarf, bring it back, reveal my forehead, even the edge of my hairline. See? But no, that is not the edge of my hairline. It is the edge of the apocalypse. You heard me right! Pull it forward to the edge of my eyebrows and we're restored to our earthly lives. Back: The flames rise. The apocalypse nears. Forward: We can resume our earthly life. Back: Doom! Annihilation! Forward: We live. Back: The netherworld. Forward: Life."

Mrs. Moghadam was nearly out of breath when she stepped off the platform. Her assistant brought her a glass of water, and they both stood among us for a moment's rest. Circled by us, she was not formidable, especially since some girls, standing on tables, towered over her. Though we could hear her clearly, she raised a megaphone to her mouth. Her big voice zinged painfully in our ears as she issued her last instructions before leaving the lunchroom: "From today's lesson, you can see how much there's still left for you to learn, and how little time we have left. It's why it would not be in your best interest to have eight full days off. I'm giving you tomorrow off. Friday and Saturday are also off as usual. But you will return to class on Sunday. And I'll see you right here on Sunday afternoon!" Amid our rumblings, she and her assistant scurried out of the hall.

"I say we kick her ass!" Mitra said, without stuttering. Rage had cured her. She turned to me and asked, "What do you say?"

Just as I was about to reply, a ball flew over my head and smashed one of the windows that opened to the yard. Then came a shout: "Down with Moghadam!"

Another student snatched a few pieces of colored chalks, stepped onto the platform, and in large print wrote the words "Down with Moghadam!" on the blackboard. Everyone cheered. Mitra bellowed again, "What do you say, everybody?"

I climbed on a table and shouted, "We've had eight days off every year. This year is no different."

Nazila completed my thought: "I say we teach the sister a lesson. Let's get out now and not come back until after the holiday."

In a stampede, we chanted, "Down with Moghadam!" and took to the schoolyard. No one led anyone. No one followed anyone. For most of 1978, kept home from school, we had studied the rebels on the streets. We knew the look and sound of a revolution. And we were, at last, making our own.

Several students climbed the plane trees alongside the yard, broke a few branches, and passed them to the rest of us. From her office, Mrs. Moghadam and her assistant stood by the window and watched. Yet no one hid. Like the nation, we threw our fists in the air and chanted. Frenzy had overtaken us. But so had an order that ruled our throng in unison. We marched from the yard into the corridor, now vibrating only to our echoes. We stormed every classroom, inscribed our slogans on the blackboard, looted what we could, and gathered ammunition—balls, brooms, markers, game rackets, and trash pails. We left no room before smashing the chalkboard eraser against the door, and thus we hoped to erase the memory of an intruder. A milky mist filled the air and showered our faces, and we, delirious girl ghosts, shone in its light. The windows crashed one after another. Never had the sound of shattering glass mended so many broken spirits. Never had mayhem brought more peace. All our lives we had been taught the virtues of behaving, and now we were discovering the importance of misbehaving. Too much fear had tainted our days. Too many afternoons had passed in silence, with us listening to a fanatic's diatribes. We were rebelling because we were not evil, we had not sinned, and we knew nothing of the apocalypse. We were rebelling for all those who had come before us and had never dared to. This was 1979, the year that showed us we could make our own destinies. We were rebelling because rebelling was all we could do to quell the rage in our teenage veins. Together as girls we found the courage we had been told was not in us.

For one spring afternoon, we, the children of Moses, freer of slaves, claimed our share of Iran's revolution. Filling the walls with graffiti, we burst the gates and flowed into the street. The walls were shaking once again, this time to the shouts of the teenage girls of Raah-e Danesh Hebrew Day School. For one afternoon, we, too, became the true daughters of the revolution. We, too, trounced tyranny, tasted the sweetness of liberty. Of victory!

8

THE DREAMERS

HOWEVER ERRATICALLY TEHRAN'S WEATHER BEHAVED IN 1982, a single storm front regularly swept through our neighborhood. That front was called Mrs. Ferdows: the human thunderstorm that occurred in reverse. First the thunder of her shriek hit, then the bolt of her image, wrapped in a print veil, tumbled. Once she struck, there was no hiding from her. And she struck every week at 4:15 A.M. on the corner of Fourteenth Street and Farahbakhsh Square, where her youngest daughter, Nazila, and I met to go mountain climbing.

She was embarrassment itself, a bust rippling at the strides of two skinny legs and a face that waned in the penumbra of its mouth. With her on the street, the neighbors delayed leaving home. The garbage man changed his route. The baker hesitated to roll up the chain shutter on his store window. Mrs. Ferdows was dramatic, yes, but at that hour, on our only day off, she was a disaster to those she had come to reprimand, to us: "Mountain climbing? Mountain climbing is for donkeys. Are you two donkeys? I'll show you such mountain climbing that ten other mountains will rise up before I'm through."

Neither Nazila nor I understood what she really meant. But that never stopped Mrs. Ferdows from saying whatever she wished: "Do you know what could happen to you in the mountains?"

Mrs. Ferdows's objection to climbing was never to the actual dangers of the sport, the possibility of falling, or getting lost on the trails. If she worried about anything slipping, it was our future opportunities, with one wrong move. And going to the mountain, she believed, was that wrong move. It could tarnish our good name. Walking alone, in pitch dark, without a parent or a chaperone, would start the rumors. Mrs. Ferdows's main concern was reputation—hers, her daughters', the people who associated with them, and, by extension, me. If Nazila had an accident, Mrs. Ferdows's second question was whether the accident had happened under innocent circumstances. Innocent, that is, in the eyes of the neighbors and acquaintances.

"She's crazy," Father always said. "What else could she be? She's the single mother of three unmarried girls."

Single mother of three unmarried girls. That phrase righted all of Mrs. Ferdows's wrongs. And the little that remained she blamed on men. Men were all supremely dangerous. They all possessed "the, the, that thing only the eunuchs in harems did not." And "that thing" made them the uncontrollable beasts she wanted us to fear. Falling prey to them took no effort. It was enough for two pairs of eyes to get tangled in a look. And there flared the spontaneous combustion, the kind of arson Mrs. Ferdows always warned us against: "Men are fire, and women, heaps of cotton. Can't put the two next to each other. Ever."

Mrs. Ferdows's husband had died when she was a young bride still in her twenties, and she had vowed never to marry again, so she could give all her attention to raising her girls. To say she had chosen to remain a widow for the sake of her daughters endeared her to a community that thrived on sacrifice. And behaving as a madwoman assured that community that the absence of a husband had not turned her into a permissive parent, and that she was watching her daughters, and protecting their virtue, with the unyielding eyes of a father.

"My Simon was a gem," Mrs. Ferdows said to Mother the first time they met. It was at the ad hoc meeting the parents of the girls of Raah-e Danesh Hebrew Day School organized after the event that came to be known as the "Passover Rebellion of 1979." Nazila and I had been identified as the leading culprits of the riot, and no amount of pleading could keep Mrs. Moghadam from expelling us. The two of us celebrated the expulsion as a divine ending to our uprising and vowed to always remember it as our "exodus." Befitting our status as the chosen pair, we became inseparable friends, and following suit, our mothers also became each other's confidantes.

But between the crisis our expulsion created and single-parenthood, Mrs. Ferdows had become terribly overprotective. She believed the job of any good mother was to keep men away from her daughters. And in doing so, she had kept everyone away. Everyone but me. I had seen her at home, when she sat in her house gown alone in the thirty-five-watt gloom of the living room lamp. Not a single watt was squandered in a household where the breadwinner was dead and the widow had to appear extravagant enough to convince the neighbors that her daughters were well provided for. Poor girls did not have the kinds of suitors Mrs. Ferdows fancied for her daughters. In that dim light, in the corner of the couch, barely blinking, not reading, radio silent, the television rarely on, she was an old spider, stuck to her own web. The gown puffed about her. The thin filaments of her feet barely reached the floor. The dark rings under her eyes deepened in the shadows. Only her nose defied the rest of her melancholy. From plastic surgery, Mrs. Ferdows had emerged with the youthful, upturned American nose she had always dreamed of. Except that her perfect American nose no longer fit her olive, often sullen Iranian face.

Despite all her clamor, Mrs. Ferdows was transparent, and I liked seeing through her. I saw her loss, the shriveled blossom of a girl still standing in the bottle of a middle-aged woman. That girl occasionally came to life. She would say something barely humorous, and suddenly a twinkle more electric than the current around her flooded her eyes. Mrs. Ferdows had lost her shot at bliss, but she never stopped trying to bring a transient version of it upon herself. To her, laughter brought prestige. Her delight was silly, aimless, like ours. Some nights she would put on her vermilion lipstick when she came to Nazila's bedroom to turn off the light. She would get impish—*Look, I'm one of you*—and say, "So tell me, Roya, which one of the boys are you eyeing?"

Boys! It was always about boys for Mrs. Ferdows. The same boys she so vehemently warned us against sounded delicious as she stood at Nazila's door, working her figure, nearly nude in her gossamer nightgown, into our pillow talk. Her contradiction, telling us that men were deadly while speaking seductively about boys, never occurred to her. Her flirtations were so inviting that they often brought me to the brink of telling. But then her Friday morning hisses echoed in my memory and saved me from giving in to her:

"You can't go mountain climbing. No good, obedient girl does. Roya can go, if she wants. She's got a father to answer for her. But you, you listen to me! You're not going anywhere."

Even the Friday morning bus driver knew what to expect as he approached Nazila and me at the station. He rarely came to a complete stop, and even when he did, it was in the middle of the street and as far away from the stand as he could. Wary of Mrs. Ferdows, he knew what we, being in the eye of her storm, did not. He understood the show of honor, the lengths to which families went to hinder their girls, to inure them to a life of restraint. The show was meant for the street, for its secretly watching eyes to see that tradition was being upheld: that those whose duty was to deny, did, and those who were denied, winced accordingly.

From the side pockets of our Islamic uniforms, we each pulled a tiny rectangular bus ticket and handed it to the driver. He tore them up and let the pieces fall into a plastic bag hanging from the dashboard. Then *he* gave us a hard look, in case we thought we were free to do as we pleased now. We skidded from the front to the back of the bus. I grasped the straps, my body trembling to his uneven accelerations, and Nazila grabbed on to me. As we settled in the back, the driver's gaze was still on us in the rearview mirror. What was it about that year that made everyone watch us all the time? Why were we suddenly at the center of everything? In the south, Saddam Hussein had declared war against Iran and was advancing through Abadan. And in Tehran, those who were not fighting Saddam were advancing on us. After the war with Iraq, the conduct of women was the nation's most consuming debate. It was the only debate that unified the sons, fathers, husbands, and brothers, religious or secular, educated or illiterate, liberal or conservative. A new law had mandated that women appear in Islamic uniform—a scarf, a long, loose-fitting overcoat, pants, and closed-toe shoes. And judging from the opinion polls that appeared in the major dailies, all citizens were unanimous:

The high school student from Qom: "I agree with the Islamic dress code because Islam, as stated by Agha, has ordered it so."

The university student from Tehran: "In Algeria, even Marxist women wore veils, and now, to fight imperialism, our women must wear the Islamic uniform so we can prove to the world that we are a sovereign nation."

The cabdriver from Isfahan: "By following the Islamic dress code, women help the nation by preventing men from being sexually stimulated."

The unemployed professor from Tehran: "Personally, I condemn the rule of the bourgeoisie in any shape or form. But as long as the modes of production are in the hands of the exploiters, women must follow the Islamic dress code to speed up the obliteration of world capitalism."

So the choice was made for us. Dressed in our Islamic uniforms and scarves in the back of the bus, we were on our way to a place away from the chaos of Tehran, to our own self-ruled territory, to the republic of rock and poetry, to the Alborz mountain range, where we could be free. The bus drove us out of the quiet alleys in the dark, and as it reached the main road, the air grew brighter, until the vista before us became the snowcapped peak of the Alborz at sunrise: the landscape that had captivated me as a child in Darband, the mountain I had wanted to hike. The bus delivered us near the foot of Alborz mountain, to the best experience of our girlhood.

Travel guidebooks to Iran trace Alborz's origin to the Larijan district, sixty-nine kilometers northeast of Tehran. They list Mount Damavand as its highest peak, four hundred meters in diameter, higher than all West Asian and European mountain peaks, and covered in snow for most of the year. Its range, they say, separates central Iran from the lush Caspian Sea area on the north. This is all true. But when the books call the Alborz "an extinct volcano of 18,600 feet high, laying behind the Tehran skyline, the record of whose last eruption no longer exists"—when I read lines like these, I lose faith in all travel books.

There was nothing extinct about our Alborz. The Damavand I knew was not a backdrop to any scene. It was all the eye could see in north Tehran. Most public places had fallen into the hands of a paramilitary force that was slowly taking hold of the city. But the Alborz belonged to no one, only to climbers. In a city of walls, fences, and barbed wires, the Alborz was gateless. Once we set foot on the steep, narrow alleys of north Tehran, we were in its territory. The air was crisper, colder. The gray Tehran palette brightened into poplar green. Loose fresh walnuts spotted the gravel. The gravel! This was Darband. The green trampoline where I left my heart as a child. This was my Darband. With every step we kicked up dust, and it sat on our clothes, on our hair, on our faces, until a thin layer of dust turned us into one majestic, khaki-colored race of the Alborz. The land of dull asphalt slept behind us. These streets were awake with the sound of the rapids that we would soon reach.

"Breathe, Roya, breathe!" Nazila said the moment the bus pulled into the square at its final stop. North Tehran ended at the

Alborz. A traveler could only turn around and go back to the city or dare to climb up and test a new dimension.

"Did you take a really good, deep breath?"

"No, Nazila. I'm postponing breathing till this afternoon. Why hurry?"

Nazila chortled. Nothing I said had to be funny at that hour. Good humor required a hot drink, a bit of blood sugar, the brain's wakeful cooperation—scarce commodities at only 5:00 A.M. But like her mother, Nazila, too, exercised auto-enjoyment. She laughed to induce happiness. Like a captive on furlough, Nazila wanted to store as much joy as fast as she could. In nearly twelve hours, we had to bring a single Friday to its knees: walk a rough trail, forget about our parents and their worries for us, flirt inconspicuously, try to understand why the religious fundamentalists were becoming so popular, rest, and be on the bus queue before sundown. The clocks in our minds had begun ticking, and Nazila was already at work winding me to performance:

"Come wash your face in this brook." She was taking off her shoes and socks, ready to immerse her feet in water, already dripping from her face and hands. Nazila was a strong believer in the curative and fortifying powers of all things natural, even dirt. But we had yet to begin our climb, and the water in which she was washing her face was the same canal water that flowed on the side of all Tehran streets.

"That's no brook, Nazila. It's canal water. People piss in it." I quickened my steps away from her.

"This clear, beautiful water? You're crazy."

Splash. Just as strongly, Nazila believed playing must never be delayed. A good time could begin anytime. Splash again. I hid like a cat afraid of a single drop.

Slowly the square awakened to the music of the local goods—the trickle of fresh, unpeeled pistachios into scalloped-edged trays, the plop of shelled walnuts into jars of salt water, the hum of juicers demanding their day's share of carrots, oranges, and cantaloupes. By the time the walnuts bloated and were placed in pyramids of twelve on the trays, the vendors would begin singing the praises of their delights. More buses pulled into the stations around the square. Within minutes, Mrs. Ferdows's apocalyptic prediction had come true. From each bus emerged a bushel of cotton, a heap of fire: other boys and girls who placed themselves in that dreaded spot: next to one another.

The core of our group consisted of nearly a dozen girls and those dangerous, delicious beasts called boys. In order of popularity, they were:

Professor Heybat, the Oxford-educated physicist who had been lured back to Iran by the excitement of the revolution. He wore bow ties, tweed jackets, and spectacles. Years of living in England had turned his Persian into what we called "dry-cleaned"—stiff, with excessive politeness. More than loving him, we loved to impress him. *Shahram* was our indisputable saint. He always mysteriously left restaurants ahead of the rest so he could pay the tab in peace and avoid our gratitude. Hence his nickname: the "Zorro of the Alborz." Until we learned that he was only a lowly bookkeeper at a small firm, everyone thought him independently wealthy. *Cyrus* was the best climber among us. While we all trudged, he hop-skipped past and flashed a smile, and said that we were almost there. His *almost* never fell short of four kilometers. *Azar* was our asthmatic artist, who panted all the way, without a single complaint, but came because the trail inspired her work.

Farifteh would have been called the loveliest among us were she not also the debater from hell. The trail exhausted us far less than she did. But where would we be without our chatterbox in the foreboding silence of the mountain? *Roya Jr.* ("Junior" so as not to confuse her with me) was easy to make laugh and therefore everyone's most favorite companion. *Isaac* was the riddle no one ever solved: Was he hideous or exotically handsome with his hooked nose and deeply set green eyes? His nickname was the Unbreakable. Despite his family's destitution, he had won full scholarship to the university and was at the top of his textile engineering class. *Eddie:* stocky, serious. Telling a joke mattered so much to him that he could never deliver an easy punch line. But everyone put up with him because he was kind and, with easy access to his father's cab, he was also the only one with wheels. *Elly,* blessed be she, our peacemaker, was heavenly.

We had all met at the Jewish Iranian Students Organization. In the early 1960s, a few dreamers, no more than four or five, not a woman among them, had envisioned it as a gathering place outside the usual haunts of Tehrani Jews. Not much was known about them, only oral legends: They were a modest few, who preferred to remain anonymous. Instead of their given Hebrew names, they went by Persian names, borrowing heroic titles from old myths, like Rostam or Zaal. They hoped to integrate Jews seamlessly in the larger society. The Pahlavis had granted Jews a life beyond the ghettos and representation in the Majles. Now it was up to them to "enlighten" everyone. Every other word they uttered was "enlightenment." Enlightenment would be the cure to the anti-Semitism that limited the Jews' professional possibilities. Enlightenment would snuff out the false hope of a better life in some distant land—their euphemism for Israel. With more than two thousand years of history in Iran, the dreamers were confident, Jews were right at home exactly where they were, as they would be nowhere else.

Those dreamers must have dreamed of my generation, because nearly two decades later, there we were, a bustling youth colony on the fifth floor of an apartment building overlooking their promised land—the intersection of the former Pahlavi Avenue and Eftekhar Alley, or the Alley of Pride. Pride was precisely what we were running on, Monday through Thursday, starting at 5:30 P.M. The opaque glass doors of the organization swung open to a hall full of smoke, hope, and at least fifty students, even on the slowest of evenings. The white walls had not been painted in years. We hardly noticed it. The floors were covered with an emetic shade of beige linoleum. We did not care. The chairs were fold-up hard metal chairs. The fluorescent light in the small library kept flickering. The net on the Ping-Pong table never stood straight. Ah, what charming imperfections! The mimeograph machine, too old for our endless supply of opinions, broke down every few days. That was our most serious problem, for it delayed the publication of our weekly bulletin and monthly magazine. But the office telephone worked. And the desk was big enough for the eight steering-committee members to huddle around and move the campaign forward—the campaign to save, first the community, then Iran, and possibly even the world. We discussed the fate of the Kurds in western Iran, the threat of food rations if the war with Iraq went on a few more weeks, or even the possibility of a coup d'état: What was Uncle Sam brewing for our nation now?

When we exhausted the domestic subjects, we moved on to the

rest of the world. We cared about suffering, no matter where it occurred, or even how long ago. Democracy had been restored to Greece, but we still held a grudge for the colonels. And what about Indonesia under General Suharto, Chile under General Pinochet, South Africa under apartheid, and—ahem—the Palestinians under the occupying Zionists? Yes, we even wanted to save the Palestinians.

"Your heads smell of parsley stew!" the elders said of us. It meant we were a crazed bunch looking for trouble. But with nearly three thousand registered members, our stew was the flavor of the day for the Jewish community. Since the revolution three years earlier, many of the community's leaders had emigrated. Yet the organization had only thrived. The country had rebelled against the shah. Now, following in the nation's footsteps, we simply rebelled. Somewhere on a plaque, our mission was stated as "raising the consciousness of the youth in the community." But we mostly enjoyed raising the blood pressure of our elders. Had we been born in London, we would have painted our nails black, dyed our hair purple, and worn studs in our noses. But being in Tehran, we dressed down and stood up to everyone. And though it would take some time to free the rest of the world, the business of the community could not be delayed: The high membership fees at congregations had to be eliminated. The south Tehran Jewish clinic needed additional funds for repairs and expansion so it could serve the poor non-Jews, too. The laws had to be adjusted so girls could receive a half of their father's inheritance instead of only one-sixth.

That simple math accounted for the force that drove us. It was what brought me to the organization every day after school. It seemed that the religious conservatives had gained momentum in the country. The organization was our bastion where we would wait them out. Besides, inside the organization, no one bothered us. In that bare hall, where girls could take off their scarves, girlhood did not seem so bleak a prospect. On Mondays, while attending meetings of the library committee, I sat next to boys and experienced nothing catastrophic. On Tuesday afternoons, in the editorial board meetings, or on Wednesdays, in the coordinating committee meetings, I saw, for the first time, female university students rebut their male counterparts and win a debate. And on Thursdays, on the organization's busiest night of the week, gathered around the refreshment table alongside boys, sipping tea, I felt a warmth faintly reminiscent of the flames Mrs. Ferdows had described. Together, we talked boldly of everything we knew nothing about. And on Friday mornings, with every dictator in power, and Uncle Sam a menace, we headed for the Alborz.

THE MOUNTAIN IS CLOSED! read a cardboard sign one Friday morning. Written in poor script, crookedly hung from the rod-iron gate of a local café, it did not have the look of an official sign. Besides, to shut down the Alborz was like damming Niagara Falls or cordoning off the Pyramids. In disbelief, we ignored it, and climbed as we did every Friday.

The trails were less crowded than usual. It was a day of mourning in the Shiite calendar. With the passing of each year after the revolution, the number of somber occasions had increased. Imams and their deputies had proliferated. But they seemed to die far more frequently than they were born, for the city was often shut down, grieving with great ceremony the death of yet another cleric.

Halfway to the summit, we stopped at a shelter to rest. To push our legs, already jittery with exhaustion, seemed ludicrous. Everyone thought the unthinkable, and the shame of it having even occurred to us flushed our cheeks. We looked at one another with knitted brows and passed the canteen, hoping the next person might be the one to say, "Let's stop here" or "Let's turn around." But everyone took a sip, and no one yielded.

We pranced around the shelter grounds. At those great heights in our rocky sanctuary, we suspended the Islamic dress code. The girls unbuttoned their uniforms and walked about with their scarves loose around their heads. Nazila had found her way to a stream and was standing on a rock, barefoot once again, washing, praising the freshness of the water, but mostly scanning other climbers. She was the only one among us who did not hide her desire for boys. So much for all the screams!

"How's the 'weather,' Nazila?" I shouted to her. *Weather* was code for the status of the attractiveness of the male climbers in her eyeshot. She crinkled her nose and narrowed her eyes. The forecast was dull. Her disappointment softened my heart. She desperately needed to be amused, or she would turn restless. So I called to her again, touched up my scarf when she looked my way, and said, "Nazila, I hate to break the news to you, but you have developed a neurotic tic. Maybe you should quit hiking for a while."

She touched up her scarf and asked, "What tic?"

I raised my hand and touched the side of my scarf and answered, "That! You just did it again."

She had touched her scarf one more time.

"There's hope for people like you. Medication can help, Nazila."

"What the hell are you talking about?"

Oblivious to my lark, she had mimicked me every time I had

tugged at my scarf. Watching someone fix her scarf in public was as infectious as yawning. Soon everyone was doing it. And after a few rounds, after I had gotten Nazila to fix her scarf with her wet hands, it was now damp through and through. Finally catching on, she darted out of the stream and charged at me. We were tangled in horseplay, which must have seemed like a tussle to Elly. She rushed over to intervene: "Don't fight!"

Nazila said, "The Alborz isn't big enough for the giraffe and me."

I threw her a kick. Elly wedged herself between us: "But see, there's good reason why you have strong disagreements."

Nazila was listening. I lunged, this time at Elly. One hand at my waist, I targeted her heart with my walking stick in my other hand, and declared, "Speak, or take thy last breath!"

Unprepared to parry, she fell to her knees and begged: "Disagreement, my lord, is only natural among the lettered. If I may be allowed to quote our father of modern poetry: 'The ignorant are harmonious. Only storm spawns discordant children.' A verse by Ahmad Shamlou, my lord! Your most beloved of poets. Will you now spare my life?"

"Elly!" I bowed and put my sword back in the sheath (under my arm had to do). "Thou art the fairest in all of Alborzstan."

By now Nazila was leaning against a rock, and with a twig, she was drawing her name in dirt. We had come together in a circle, quiet with contentment. This was the moment that made all the troubles—the early rise from bed, the howls of Mrs. Ferdows, the driver looking at us askance, the trudge up the trail—worthwhile. Below us, the city, the homes with our parents in them, looked shrunken with sleep. But the tingle in our skin, the buzz in our muscles, the floating sensation in our heads, signaled the flow of wakefulness at its best in us. Our motley bundles of cheese, olives, bread, herbs, and fruits made the rounds. And the inevitable was about to begin: first the joint singing of a few folk songs, then reciting poetry. Along with the food, the canteen, and the extra socks, we always packed a few pages of reading material: a poem, a song, sometimes an antiwar leaflet that had been slipped to the university students among us. Carrying those few pages made us all feel we still had some freedom; we still had some privacy left to us, and could carry what we wished in our bags.

Shahram suggested that someone recite a *ghazal* by Hafez. But Isaac objected:

"You want Hafez, my friend, you go next door and sit with the senior citizens. Follow the signs for the Local Assembly of Suckers Worshiping the Unidentifiable Muse Club. We, here, aren't your crowd."

This could have been the start of a shouting match if Azar had not seized the opportunity: "I dare anyone to rise to a declamation match of Forough Farrokhazad, the mother of our modern poetry. Let's hear it, everyone."

There was a round of clapping hands.

"Allow me." I bowed once again, then tapped on one end of my walking stick, held it in front of my mouth—*testing, testing, one, two, three*—and began:

> *"I know a sad little fairy*
> *who lives in an ocean*
> *and ever so softly*
> *plays her heart into a wooden flute*
> *a sad little fairy*
> *who dies with one kiss each night*
> *and is reborn with one kiss each dawn."*

Farifteh interjected, "Get lost! Every schoolgirl knows this one."

Waving a new edition of Forough's poetry in the air, Azar said, "Let me read to you, my dear plebeians, from here. It's the newest edition."

The gazes were fixed on Azar as she skimmed the lines for a few moments and, in a puzzled tone, finally said, "Either I've gone crazy or this is a defective copy."

"Why don't you just read?"

"Well, it's missing words." She brought the book close to her eyes and strained to read a random stanza aloud:

> *"One can shout,*
>   *—in the fakest tone*
>   *in all insincerity:* I love you!
> *One can lie,*
>   *in a lover's embrace,*
>   *with two big hard, dot, dot, dot."*

"Hey, what do you mean dot, dot, dot?"

Exasperated, Azar said, "Well, exactly. The words are missing. I have bought a defective copy."

Nazila was fully engaged at last: "Well, let's fill in the blank, shall we? Two boobs? Two buns? Two balls?"

"Somebody please stop the advance of Nazila's imagination!"

Eddie took the book and carefully leafed through the pages. In a few seconds, his eyes had a look of eureka in them. He silenced everyone: "Ladies and gentlemen, welcome to the new era of censorship, ayatollah style."

The book was now in my hand. And Eddie was right. It had

been censored. In every poem, there were words missing. Cyrus reached for his backpack. He whispered that he had the uncensored text of the poem written in longhand, and he was about to bring it out, when we were interrupted:

"Did you not see the 'Mountain Is Closed' sign?" a teenager in army fatigues said as he leaped and landed on a rock above us. In his left hand, he held a Kalashnikov. He placed one foot a little higher and rested the end of his rifle on his thigh—the final touch to the pose of one in command.

Cyrus found the courage to speak. He explained that the sign had seemed odd: "We ignored it, because the closing of the mountain was unprecedented."

Unprecedented was the wrong word, because the young man reached for his walkie-talkie and called for additional "backup." "Unprecedented," he said, belonged to the Pahlavi era. These were new times. The revolution was making its own precedents. Anything was possible now, even shutting down the Alborz if it was what the imam ordered or the revolution needed. According to the needs of his revolution, the Alborz could be shut down, if necessary. According to ours, it was unthinkable.

Within minutes, three other men arrived. They knew the trails well and had reached us quickly. They moved over the rocks better than gazelles. Though they were far fewer than us, their casual conduct, their erect postures in their uniforms, the ease with which they held their guns in one hand as if they were holding walking sticks, the way the noise from their walkie-talkies filled the open air, made us feel surrounded by a battalion. In the heart of our republic, in our sanctuary, in the heart of the great Alborz, we had become captives.

They followed us down the mountain. A bus was waiting for

us once we reached the foot. We were ordered to get on it. They followed in their own car. Here was our only chance to get a story straight before being questioned by them. It was also our last chance to do something about the pages we had on us. Cyrus and Shahram exchanged a few quick words. Leaving his pack with Shahram, Cyrus walked to the front of the bus. Standing inches away from the rearview mirror, he blocked the driver's view of the cabin. To ease the driver's suspicion, he began to play the part of the honorable guide trying to calm the minds of the group in his charge. He said that this was all a big mistake or misunderstanding. Surely once we got to the headquarters, it would take only seconds to clear the matter.

While Cyrus diverted the driver's attention, the leaflets and the poems had been collected. Fortunately, it added up to a slim pile. Our bags were likely to be inspected at the headquarters. Any trace of literature such as what we carried would easily implicate us in an anti-revolutionary plot. The boys passed their material to the girls. It was unlikely that a female paramilitary member would be present at the headquarters to body-search us. And the male guards would not touch us. The pile was handed to Nazila and me. As the youngest in the group, we had the best chance to be let go. We took the pages and shoved them in our clothes.

The headquarters was an elegant mansion in northern Tehran, where the Pahlavis and their inner circle had kept residence. We were guided through a passageway of marble columns. Azar's asthma had attacked. I knew without even talking to Nazila that she was worrying about these next few hours, and about the evening, when she would arrive home, long past her curfew. Mrs. Ferdows had no sympathy for crises that could have been avoided, if only her advice had been heeded.

Beyond the columns, an indistinct black presence lurked at the window of the main building. Within a few steps, we could tell that it appeared to be the outline of a veiled woman. For us, it had only one meaning: a woman was on hand to conduct a body search on us.

Nazila turned ashen. With only seconds to think, she shouted, "Bathroom, please!" The guard pointed her to a door with a stick-figure drawing of a woman hanging on it. Even the stick figure's head was covered by a scarf.

I realized what she was about to do. And I, too, asked for permission to use the bathroom. As we passed each other, Nazila warned, "Don't flush them! They may not go down." And each of us disappeared into a stall.

In the main hall of the headquarters, the group had been lined up against the back wall. Cyrus was speaking to a man who seemed to be in charge. He and Cyrus looked very much alike. Both had jet-black hair. Both were soft-spoken. Both sets of eyes were invisible behind the thick lenses of their glasses. Only one had shaved and the other had not. In another era, they could have been twins, separated by a desk. But in our era, the beard on the face of the seated man erased all the similarities between them.

When I walked in, the bearded man was enumerating to Cyrus all the many violations we had committed. First, we had violated the Alborz closure sign. Next, we were a group not married or related by blood, and by socializing with one another we had violated the Islamic morality code. Finally, by taking off their scarves, the girls had violated the Islamic dress code.

I joined the group and took my place next to Nazila. When I

had settled in my spot, she whispered in my ear, "I don't know if it was the buns, the boobs, or the balls I just swallowed, but they tasted awful."

A loud laugh escaped from me. The bearded man looked up. He stretched out his arm, an angry officer guiding rush-hour traffic, and waved me to him. I walked up to his desk. He tapped his pen against the telephone and, without meeting my eyes, asked, "What's so funny?"

"Nothing. I'm sorry. It's just . . . you know, girl talk. I'm very sorry."

He hooted: "Sorrry, are you? Open up your bag!"

I did. He removed all the contents of my bag and was holding it upside down, shaking it in the air. Pieces of lint fell on his face. His assistant was reading through the only notebook I always carried with me—my diary, my poetry book, all in one. With his eyes fixed on my writing, his assistant said, "So you must be missing your masters pretty badly these days."

"I don't follow what you're saying."

The assistant told his superior, "No disrespect to you, but she thinks we are a couple of idiots here."

Then he began reading aloud a passage from my notebook: " 'Our king of kings, may he be eternal, in his shadow . . .' "

He recited other lines facing his superior. He was quoting the Pahlavi national anthem from my notebook. According to the assistant, I was a royalist sympathizer, and the evidence of his accusation was in my own handwriting. But I had never seen the text. So I asked, "May I see, ah, mister?"

"Mister. She calls me mister."

The sardonic tone was meant for me, but he was addressing his superior. I should have called him "brother." But I could not. He dropped the notebook on the desk. I browsed the pages. The anthem and several other Pahlavi-era songs were indeed in my notebook but not in my handwriting. The man had unglued some old pages from the cover. The notebook had belonged to my brother Javid when he was a Boy Scout, and all of his Boy Scout training notes, even the instructions on how to tie various knots, were there. Not wanting to tear up the pages, I had taped them onto the cover and went on to use the remaining blank sheets. Then I forgot about them altogether. I explained the matter to the men. Each gave a sarcastic nod and continued to inspect the rest of my belongings. Wrapped in several tissues inside a paper bag was a sanitary napkin. The assistant could not make out what it was at first. Before he opened the bag, I said, "Feminine items." Quickly he withdrew his hand and muttered something under his breath. In the clutter on the desk there was also a piece of writing in Hebrew. That, too, I could not remember. But I averted my eyes, so as not to call attention to something he may have missed.

"What is this gibberish?" The assistant pointed to the text.

Instead of handing it to me, he left it on the table for me to pick up. Religious observance prohibited a man from making direct physical contact with a woman. I picked up the text. It was a "traveler's prayer," something Mother always put in my bags for good luck. I told them so.

"Are you a Jew?" the assistant asked. But before I could answer him, he turned to his superior and exclaimed, "She's a Jew."

The first sign of a cheery expression came over the assistant's face, and suddenly buoyant, he said, "Jews are cowards. They never get mixed up in politics. Ha! And we thought we had got ourselves a pack of leftists or royalists." He threw the notebook on the desk and signaled to me to gather my things. "Wait a minute. Are you all Jews?"

I nodded. The assistant asked his superior, "Since when do Jews know how to climb mountains?"

The superior recited a passage in Arabic, in which I heard the title "Moses the shepherd," and the assistant nodded his head in acknowledgment. Their faces had finally brightened. The assistant gave me a knowing look. His eyes met mine for the first time. With greater courage, I said, "Yes, brother, we're all children of Moses."

Within minutes we were on the street, rushing to find buses and taxis back to the city.

That night, Professor Heybat offered to drive Nazila and me. We hesitated. The embarrassment of an encounter between the physicist from Oxford and Mrs. Ferdows, sure to be waiting on the stoop, had to be measured against exhaustion. It was too dark, too late on a Friday evening, and we had been through too much. We accepted his offer. At Farahbakhsh Square, we thanked the professor and asked to be dropped off. But his Persian manners, compounded by British etiquette, would not yield unless he saw us to our doors. The encounter was imminent.

Long past our curfew, we arrived at Nazila's door. But Mrs. Ferdows was not in sight. Overjoyed, Nazila dashed out, and the professor headed in the direction of my house. As we approached my block, I spotted Mother standing in the middle of the street. How odd! Mother was always gracious, and never one for making scenes.

The professor pulled up to our door. Mother walked up to the car and tapped on the driver's-side window. He rolled down the window and greeted her: "It is an unparalleled honor to make your acquaintance, Mrs. Hakakian."

"Honor you speak of? Is this the kind of time your own mother and sister come home?"

Honor, mother, sister, all in one sentence, as a reply to his simple greeting puzzled Professor Heybat. Fortunately, his Persian was not good enough to know that he had just been insulted. Instead, he was about to tell Mother about the daily routine of his female relatives, when through clenched teeth, I begged her to say good-bye. I tugged at her dress and pulled her through the doorway. The professor wished us a good night and drove away.

Inside the house, I discovered that the scene had been master-minded by Mrs. Ferdows. After sundown she had come to our door, but not upstairs, and begun screaming from the street as Mother and Father stood at the kitchen window. When Father pleaded with her to be quiet, she had questioned his ability to raise a girl. Then she had demanded that Father stop me from having any contact with Nazila. To this, he had simply said, "As you aptly put it yourself, I cannot raise my daughter the way a father should, so I encourage you to stop your daughter from associating with mine." His reply had only set her screaming again. She had exhausted my parents' patience and driven Mother to the street. And Mrs. Ferdows finally did the same to me, once I had heard the account.

I stormed out and began walking to Nazila's house. It was after midnight. The streets were dead. Nazila opened the door with a smile, happier to receive me than to wonder why I was there at all. It was my turn to stand at Mrs. Ferdows's bedroom door. I ordered her to get out of bed. No reply. I walked into the bedroom and turned on the lights. She rose up halfway in bed with her usual impish grin and said softly, "It's late, Roya. Can't this wait till tomorrow?"

I flickered the light. The answer was negative. To assure her that I had no intention of leaving, I walked into every room and turned on all the lights in the apartment. Now she had to get up, if only to save electricity. I was through with good, obedient, honorable, and had had it with virtue and praise. As for reputation, well, to hell with reputation: "Don't ever, ever come to my house or upset my parents again. Never. Because if you do . . ."

I faltered, coming to grips with my own limitations: "You! You embarrassed me to pieces. Don't ever do that again."

Nazila, silent and shocked, watched me. Mrs. Ferdows stared into my eyes, as if to size up my seriousness. She was intuitive, and knew when to relent. She mumbled, "Okay, okay," a few times. In the vocabulary of such an unyielding woman as she, "okay" was a synonym for "sorry."

The wind had picked up, but lightly so. Walking home, I felt the breeze soothe my cheeks. I lifted a hand to brush a lock of hair out of my eyes. Did I really just do that? My scarf had fallen to my shoulders, and for the first time in months, the wind was blowing through my hair. That sweaty, matted web, which lay under the scarf for most of my waking hours, still had life, and bounced. Between me and the brightly lit square, there was half a block where I could safely walk in the dark with my head exposed. The scarf sat on my shoulders. This was not a choice, but a concession to my mutinous hands. They were cured of their tic, and refused to reach and pull the scarf back over my head. Half a block only, I negotiated with the rebel within. This half-block was our own neighborhood, a portion of the street that, like Alborz, fell within our own free republic.

Or did it?

No, it did not. My lingering terror from all the hours at the headquarters, my final outburst at Nazila's home, had pushed the clouds away from my awareness: there were no republics. And we were not free. The city had ceased to be ours. And today we had surrendered the Alborz. The organization was not a bastion. It was a place where Jews gathered. It was a ghetto and therefore irrelevant. We were insignificant. If we had been left in relative peace at the organization, it was because the authorities had no regard for us. The men at the headquarters were not replicas of the other comical extremist who took over our school once. They were not comical at all. They were extremists with telephone lines, walkie-talkies, and desks inside which they locked stamps and letterheads that could seal our destinies.

A day that began at 4:00 A.M. had just ended after midnight— a day denser than only one. Deep in this day was a feeling of aging, not by growing but by diminishing. I tried to think further, to find wisdom in the experience. But everything blended together, into a chaos. My mind, just as mutinous as my hands, had begun its own rebellion. It refused thinking. All thoughts, all memories gathered to forge a single feeling: Fury!

9

1984

THEN I LEANED OVER HIS SERENE FACE AND WHISPERED IN his ear, "Agha! Agha, are you awake?" He did not open his eyes. He said nothing. The heater behind his bed was hissing, and I thought he might not have heard me. I lowered my head again, so close to his that I could smell the antibiotic on his breath: "Agha, can you hear me?"

He grunted. A few coughs followed, each a gurgle of phlegm. His sounds were haltingly electric, and I thought I must not bring my head so near a head of such holy stature. Who knew what he was capable of, even bedridden? His next grunt came as he pointed to the Koran on the tray at the foot of his bed. I took it to mean that he wanted the book and slid it under his hand, still eager to grasp what his eyes could no longer behold. But he grunted louder, and I lowered my face to his wrinkled lips.

"Read," he gasped, "in my name, in the name of the ayatollah who brought you the revolution."

"But Agha," I pleaded, "I'm a girl. I'm a Jew. I'm dirty. I must not recite the holy book."

He opened his eyes, and, though terribly weak, they still refused to make another's contact. His eyebrows, thick and black, had kept their old defiant arch. His face looked gaunt under the beard that eclipsed his neck. His austerity, even the sternness of his mouth, was still in place. So was the contempt in his tone. I eased the book out of his grip. With another grunt, he tilted his head to the left. He was looking at the skullcap that had slipped to his shoulder. I placed it back on his head. His head looked so ordinary now that it had shed the halo of the turban. The cap collapsed again, as if there were no skull underneath to fill it. Where had that seditious head gone?

He reached for my collar and pulled me to him: "What does 'ayatollah' mean?"

I murmured, "Sign of God!"

"Read, then, in his name!" he ordered, and shut his eyes.

The book was in my left hand, while my right rummaged through my bag searching for the syringe. I declaimed the only passage of the Koran I knew by heart: *"Dhalek al-ketabo la ray ba fee . . ."*

Serenity swept over his face. I rested the book against the bed. Both hands free, I reached into my bag once more and assembled the syringe. Then I snapped off the narrow glass top of the vial and inserted the needle into it. His index finger kept drawing a circle in the air, but his body was otherwise still. "Repeat!" the circles commanded, and I obliged. *"Dhalek al-ketabo la ray ba fee . . ."*

I watched the liquid rise in the syringe: 100 cc, 200 cc, 300 cc, 400 cc. That had to be enough. I withdrew the syringe and pressed the piston to force out the air. The time had come. With one swift move, one that I had practiced on my pillow a hundred times, I punctured the gorged vein under his paper-thin skin. His finger circled no more.

With every drop of cyanide I injected into him, his complexion darkened like a bruise breaking outward onto the surface of his skin. *Tsss!* The sizzling sound of his flesh shrinking in a venomous fire entwined with the sound of the heater hissing. He was looking me in the eye now, and I, certain that these were his last moments, stared boldly back at him. Suddenly he heaved himself to a half-seated position and bellowed, *"Allahu-Akbar!"*

That sound still echoing in the air, a kick broke the door open. Two guards, cocking their Kalashnikovs, screamed, *"Ist!"* And I heard *Pop! Pop! Pop!* Blood began to stream down my arms, dripping off my fingers, spreading over Agha's chest. One of the men shouted, "She is about to defile the imam!" But it was too late. I lifted my head, gave them a last, triumphant look, and died.

Throughout 1984, Roya, the dream, had only nightmares.

At least once a night, I murdered Ayatollah Khomeini. He died by poisonous injection each time, but my fate varied: On nights that the air raid siren shrieked through the morning hours and the Iraqi missiles fell on the city, the imam did not die right away; his joints cracked and he writhed in agony to his last breath. On quiet nights, ecstatic crowds stormed the room, lifted me, a heroine, upon their shoulders, and carried me to the streets.

The war with Iraq was in its fourth year. Though the military had driven the invading army back to the original borders, the imam wanted no truce. There would be no peace, he vowed, until our troops had freed the city of Baghdad and gone to conquer Jerusalem, where he would lead a prayer at the Temple Mount. With Iran intact once again, continued fighting no longer seemed a patriotic duty, only a prolonged exercise of the imam's favorite sport.

His Holiness's gaze was upon us everywhere. His rosy-cheeked portraits were painted larger than life on all signboards. And my imagination encountered each rendition like a guillotine, severing, then filling every unpleasant void with the imam's disembodied parts. And I felt no guilt. In the boiling pots on our stove, his head stewed. From the empty hooks in butcher shops, his carcass dangled. *Ribs, anyone?* When he appeared on television, I examined the audience, hoping to spot an assassin. My murderous fantasy had become so overpowering that I began to ponder it: Did I have the heart to kill anyone? Oh, him I could kill! Though not in a bloody encounter. Nor did I trust my nerves around flailing limbs (I had proved a disappointment as a fisher one summer when, upon seeing a squirming fish at the end of my line, I threw the rod into the water and ran away in tears). A quick, clean, poisonous injection was a reasonable solution. Murdering him was the only solution, given the magnitude of my desperation, given the magnitude of the city's desperation.

I could say desperation was the city itself. But that would be assuming the city was alive at all. It was not. The city as I knew it, as Uncle Ardi knew it, had died. That city, denounced as "decadent," had been annihilated. The cosmopolitan beat around Tehran University was hushed. The campus was now the official mosque, where the president led thousands in prayer every Friday. The bookstores displayed only religious or college preparatory texts. Cabarets and liquor stores had been looted and shut down. The war and international sanctions had imposed severe food rations. Most restaurants had closed or offered a limited menu. Mosques were the most popular hubs, not because the people's faith in religion had grown—in fact, it had diminished—but because mosques were the distribution centers where people stood on line for hours to buy the staples that had become delicacies: milk, eggs, bread, cooking oil, on good days even stockings and sanitary napkins.

The city's walls had turned into one endless mural to the rancor the imam and his disciples spewed in every speech: "America can't do a damn thing! . . . Let us praise that thirteen-year-old boy who straps a bomb to his body and throws himself in front of the Iraqi tanks . . . America worse than England, England worse than America, the Soviet Union, the worst of all . . . I will murder, I will murder whoever murdered my brother! . . . Come bury our martyrs, O' Mahdi our Messiah, O' Mahdi our Messiah!"

With hundreds of thousands killed in the war, grief and vengeance were the only feelings the public could safely express. It was all that we felt, anyway. With every street renamed, the city's grid had become a map of morbidity, pointing to doom in all directions. Every address was an intersection of death and an ayatollah. Could a wedding, a birthday, an anniversary, really be a celebration of life at the corner of Ayatollah Kashani and Martyr

Bazmi; the junction of Martyr Rajayee and the Zahra Cemetery Highway; the intersection of Martyr Heshmat and Martyr Chamran? Driving to destinations of the dead, walking on roads leading to them, the living had become but ghosts.

Yearning for the memories of the old, familiar places, I kept buying maps of the city. One in particular, Map #255, touted itself "the most complete atlas of the new Tehran, planned, produced, and lithographed by the Geographical and Cartographic Society." On its upper right corner a zip code, telephone, and fax number appeared, anything to impress an unknowing customer. Though I knew nothing about cartography, I went about examining this map. I knew Tehran. Why be intimidated? Under a magnifying glass, I looked and looked for Saba Street or Alley of the Distinguished. But on the map of the "new Tehran," there was no sign of my old neighborhood, the schools where I had studied, the places I had known. Everything was either renamed or dropped. Instead of a magnifying glass, I thought, I ought to hold a pen. Instead of maps, I ought to buy notebooks, for those cartographers, geographers, and their fancy societies could not be trusted. And I had to record, commit every detail to memory, so I could do in words what the cartographers had not done in their maps: attest to the existence of a time, an alley, and its children whose traces were on the verge of vanishing.

To cleanse the city of any lingering "decadence" of the old monarchs, the imam declared the greatest jihad of all: the one against the "self." He expected each citizen to master, by way of annihilation, every desire. To assure that every Iranian fulfilled that order, the Ministry for the Promotion of Virtue and Prevention of Vice was created. In khaki-colored Toyota SUVs, the guards prowling the streets in fours arrested men in short sleeves, women with a hint of makeup, girls whose bangs peeked from under their scarves. All lines that had once separated the citizenry—age, gender, even religion—paled. A new line, invisible but terribly palpable, was drawn. On one side of it, *they* stood. On the other, *we*.

They were the ones with guns. *We* were the ones without. *They* had the power to arrest us, on a whim. Woeful was their rule of claw! *They* had long beards or stubbly faces. *We* shaved. *They* donned collarless shirts. *We* put on ties. *They* wore their black veils as naturally as a second skin, held the two corners by their teeth, leaving their hands free to frisk us. *We* were the ones, forced under veils, mummified. *They* were the superfluous salt-and-pepper turbans in every landscape. *We* were the bitter, watching. *They*, poorly educated *mostaz'afeen,* were suspicious of anyone wearing prescription glasses. *We* were the ones with weak eyes. *They* began their speeches in the name of Allah. *We* began ours with good old God. *They* called themselves the "faithful." *We* called ourselves Iranians. *They* addressed one another and strangers as "brother" or "sister." *We* went by "Mr." and "Mrs." *They* locked away the Matisse and Picasso nudes in museum basements. *We* were artists, aghast. *They* apprehended anyone with a cello, guitar, or violin case in hand. *We* were musicians mourning the ban on music. *They* forbade dance of any kind. *We* were ballerinas, every limb in mutiny. *They* crashed parties and sniffed the mouths of guests for the smell of "sin," of alcohol. *We* were connoisseurs burying our few remaining vintages in the garden. *They* were the heavy sleepers. *We* lent each other Valium. *They* sent their sons, fathers, and brothers to the war fronts wearing a plastic key to Eden's gates for a dog tag. *We* dodged the draft, if we could. *They* referred to their veterans with two or four missing limbs as the "fortunate forty percent or eighty percent heroes." *We* referred to them as double amputees and quadriplegics. *They* were the overnight entrepreneurs eager to export their brand of salvation first to Baghdad, next to Jerusalem, and then to the rest of the world. *We* only wanted Tehran back.

If *they* relented at all, it was at night, when the blacked-out city reeled under the bombs. During the first years of the war, we did not take the air raid siren seriously. Instead of going to the bomb shelters, Father and I, the local reconnaissance team, rushed to the rooftop of our rented apartment building. He watched for bursts in the sky to figure out what places had been hit and how badly. I listened for the sounds, the latest news and jokes the neighbors exchanged: "There was this Hezbollah guy who goes to the war front and gets hit by shrapnel one day. Do you know what happens to him, Mr. Hakakian?"

Not knowing the new neighbors well, Father cautiously shook his head no.

"Well, his right arm flies off into a trench, and he's about to bleed to death, when a bright apparition riding on a white horse picks up the arm, places it back in the joint, and *voilà!* The gleeful soldier begs, 'O glorious vision, do tell me, are you the Messiah our imam promised?' 'No, my son,' the apparition replies, 'I'm a proud representative of Crazy Glue Inc.'"

Father would pinch me to stop me from laughing, while another neighbor would point to the sky and say, "I don't see anyone's picture in the moon, do you?"

A few expletives would follow.

Still, amazingly, life moved forward. Mother kept our home. Father kept teaching. I studied. I was a senior at a non-Jewish high school, once again a newcomer. The owners of our last apartment sold the building and we were forced to move to another neighborhood. By then, most Jewish and Christian schools had been shut down or taken over by Mrs. Moghadam and her protégés, the notorious "Holy Cleaner-Uppers," as they had come to be known among the minority communities. I did not care terribly about the fates of those schools. I was happy to be where I was, in the largest school I had ever attended, lost among hundreds of girls: the little black fish at last in the sea. Most refreshing of all was to meet people who were still grounded, not contemplating leaving Iran, as so many Jews were.

Adjusting to my new surroundings went smoothly at first. But a few days into the new school year, non-Muslim students were ordered to leave the class for the Koran and religious studies hours. When we all returned, a certain strangeness had set in. Immediately after those periods, a bit of warmth had dissipated from our midst. The easiness of our conversations, our playful tugs at one another's scarves, our indiscriminate horseplay, had diminished. Our Muslim classmates hesitated to share in our lunches. And I began to feel that something the class was being taught in our absence was poisoning our friendships. Or was I imagining things? Father always said that being a "Roya" made me prone to dreaming. But two months into the academic year, the principal summoned the student body to the schoolyard for an urgent announcement. There, our principal, looking crestfallen, said that according to a new regulation, non-Muslim students could only use designated water fountains and bathrooms. Aha, Father! What do you say to that? And he who had once lived

through such a time and made an art of circumventing segregation said only this: "Eh, they come and go, these lunatics!"

Lunacy was one of the characteristics of that Orwellian year.
Another regulation mandated that all non-Muslim business owners display signs in their windows: THIS STORE IS OPERATED BY A
NON-MUSLIM. Restaurateurs were most affected. But in the end
everyone was hurt, since the war had long slowed the economy.
Profits aside, the decree was a blow to the morale of the minority professionals. True to the Hippocratic oath, Jewish doctors
and nurses in small cities rushed to treat the wounded soldiers
but were spurned by them, for however critical their condition,
they wished not to be touched by "unclean" Jews. What I and the
other young dreaming Jews believed the revolution had buried
for good, the war had resurrected. Such rejection was a kind we
had only heard about from our parents. The soldiers preferred to
bleed, and the small towns lost their Jewish professionals to
Tehran, and Tehran was slowly losing them to the rest of the
world. Even Father, who still contended that the days of the
mullahs were numbered, finally submitted our passports for
renewal, though "only as a precautionary measure."

Within a month, Mother's request was denied. Mine was held
over for "further consideration," and Father's passport was confiscated.

Father began consulting friends. Earlier that year, a large delegation of Jews had paid the imam a visit at his northern Tehran residence. Now Father wondered if the confiscation had anything to
do with his refusal to go along. Perhaps it had been a trial by the
authorities, he thought, to identify Jews who were loyal to the

imam. Perhaps only those who made the pilgrimage were granted passports. Guilt-ridden, he made call after call to inquire about the details of that event. But everyone who had paid Agha the visit believed Father was worrying for no good reason. In every call he heard the same: "Rest assured, Hakakian! This was not the same ayatollah we met in Qom in 1979."

Unlike the warm welcome the six Jewish leaders had received five years earlier, this group had been treated like a stray herd. At seven separate security stations, Agha's men had removed everything, down to the handkerchiefs from their pockets, and conducted a thorough body search, combed through the visitors' heads, and fingered them in unmentionable places. The impromptu displays of Iranian modesty and hospitality, standing face-to-face before Agha and refusing to sit until he had, were now only a memory. After the laborious searches, the visitors had been guided into a sterile meeting room and were seated on the floor. Instead of the imam, they were met by another slew of handlers, who spent the next hour instructing them on how to welcome Agha: when to sit, bow, or rise, when to throw their fists into the air, chant "Allahu-Akbar," and how many times and when to give the final shout: "We are all your soldiers, O Khomeini. We all obey your orders, O Khomeini."

When the imam finally arrived, he sat not across from the visitors, but above them on a balcony surrounded by armed guards. No, Father had not missed the beat of opportunity this time. This was beyond him.

Mother had only her brothers to turn to for help. Aunt Zarrin and Uncle A.J. had gone to America to be with Farah, whose troubles with Jahan had only worsened. After breaking Farah's arm in a domestic fight, Jahan had been taken into police custody and she, who desperately wanted a divorce, was caring for her three children.

As he always did in bad times, Father turned inward. He locked himself in a room for days to forge his own brand of remedy: compose a poem for the passport officials! He wrote a sonnet about redemption through the study of knowledge and piety as prescribed in the teachings of Imam Ali. The poem ended: "Once Haghnazar became a follower of Ali, a drop he became in the sea of the pious."

Thrilled by his creation, he smiled the smile of a great schemer on the verge of pulling a most vicious trick on his unknowing adversaries. For Father to cast himself as a Jew who admired a leading Shiite figure was the zenith of deceit. The ultimate act of corruption in his life: to sing an imam's praise to get ahead. God save us all from duplicitous headmasters!

I regretted the heartache the passport ordeal caused my parents, but I was pleased that it made emigrating an even more remote possibility for us. It had taken five years, but finally I had arrived at the largest school I had ever attended, and in a year I could apply to the university. If only by instinct, I sensed that I was on the brink of one of the most important experiences of my life. And I learned, quite soon, to call that experience Mrs. Arman.

How can I best describe her? Here is the very first image I saw of her: a leg kicking the air, falling, then the other, lifting to do the same, at the door of our classroom. Ah, yes! Her kicking legs in beige pants and black shoes!

The leg carried on without her body following. She was hiding behind the wall, waiting to hear our scattered chuckle merge in a big burst of laughter. Once she had everyone's attention, she appeared at the door: a heavyset, middle-aged, female Harpo Marx. Her scarf pulled so far forward, she had to throw her neck back to see us. Then she strutted in, looking at us in a perfectly tilted profile, in perfect silence. What pomposity the struts conveyed, the silliness of the exaggerated pull of the scarf, which had revealed the back of her head, undid: *So good a Muslim, I even cover my eyes and gladly trip myself walking!* We giggled, watching with anticipation what she would do next as we stood at attention for the "You may sit!" that she would not say. Her prolonged silence, punctuated by the racket she created with every step—dropping her big black purse on the desk, picking up a piece of chalk only to throw it over her shoulder at the board, plopping the books under her arm on a front bench—made for the most hilarious debut by a teacher. Then she pulled her scarf back slightly, her gaze moving from one face to the next until she had examined each, and spoke at last: "You're the ugliest bunch I've ever had." Her honey-colored eyes, her mouth brimming with a mischief even more youthful than our own, bestowed all the sweetness a look ever can.

On the first day of classes, several of Mrs. Arman's old students—her groupies, as we later learned—came to prepare us for the "Arman phenomenon." Even as they drilled us on the six basic Arman facts, they warned that there was no preparing for so exceptional a teacher: "One: You only think you are in a Persian literature and composition class, but in fact you are undergoing Armanization. Two: Armanization is impossible to define but easy to quantify—tougher than physics, biology, chemistry, and trigonometry combined. Three: Never allow the 'Arman fun' to fool you into thinking she's an easy grader. The last highest mark she gave was a nineteen back in 1971, and she reserves twenty for God only. Four: Never quote a poet, writer, or literary scholar unless you have memorized the exact words, down to the punctuation. She belongs to an old lineage of Persian-language masters, editors of grammar, stylebooks, and dictionaries, so words mean the world to her. Five: Know your place and count your blessings within the Arman aura. She once ran a much bigger 'ship,' but for unmentionable reasons she is now just a teacher. Six: Never ask Mrs. Arman about the unmentionable reasons mentioned in number five."

"There are two kinds of girls," Mrs. Arman went on to say, standing at the window, her eyes fixed on the building across the street, "pretty ones and ones who will have to go to college. The only exception to that truism is standing in front of you."

A master at timing, she paused just long enough for her grandiose remark to set in before adding, "Judging by your sorry state, you will need to work very hard to not land over there."

There was the building she kept tilting her head toward, the Marriage Foundation, a state-funded matchmaking outfit, across the street from our school, established to find wives for the disabled war veterans and widows of the "martyrs." "But we've got a shortage of men and you're too ugly anyway, so you'd not have much luck even over there. You're stuck here with me, and in my bag of tricks, I've got only literature."

Within a couple of weeks, she had nicknamed us all. (I had been anointed with "Toothpick.") We laughed with her at ourselves. What her bag of tricks revealed was delight, a reprieve from the society that had closed in on us.

"This thing could save you, my adorable morons, if you only keep reading. You know, you can always get your revenge on the page. Literature isn't just another subject. It's your cure." *Panacea* was what she called the force that had kept me from throwing myself off the rooftop a few years earlier. What I had known only in solitude, Mrs. Arman made public: literature.

She gave us a shelter, a *here* against *there*. She never sat behind her desk, away at the other end of the class. She walked through our rows and did to us what we dared to do only to one another in the schoolyard. She transgressed the grim boundaries the uniforms were intended to draw. She defied our uniforms. She touched us. She tugged at the backs of our scarves, and when they dropped to our shoulders, she chided, "Sisters, can you not read the slogan on the wall over *there?*"

On the wall of the Marriage Foundation, Mrs. Arman's perpetual source of humor, a slogan read: "Behind every woman without a veil stands a man without balls!"

We laughed at her witty allusions, at her disguised opposition to the slogan, at the scarves on our heads. Then she would move to the next aisle, stand behind one of us, reach for the shirt under our uniforms, turn a collar over, and glance at the label: "Fancy! Tell me, Toothpick, where did you steal this from?"

"My brothers sent it from America, ma'am."

"America, the Great Satan?"

"The one and only, ma'am."

"How many brothers have you shipped there, Toothpick?"

"Three."

"Are they as ugly as you?"

"Much uglier, ma'am."

She put her glasses on to examine the label closely: "The United Colors of Benetton. Hmm. You know, Toothpick, things like this don't impress me."

"Only good writing does."

"You think you're quick, Toothpick, do you not?"

"I think you do, too, ma'am."

Mrs. Arman's greatest compliments were her wordless ones. When acknowledging a worthy exchange, she cast a last tender look from the corner of her eyes and moved on to the next subject: "Everyone, turn your attention to the handout I gave you. The poem by 'Anonymous' from the sixth century. It's really an elegy in the voice of an ordinary citizen suffering at the hands of the savage occupiers led by Genghis Khan. Look at the opening line: 'Death too will fall upon your world, so will famine upon the bounty of your laden tables.' Who can interpret this timeless line?"

Seeing our hands in the air, she was assured that her reference was not lost on us. So she would move to the next line, stand behind the next student, tug at the next scarf, turn the next collar over, lay her book on a head or her hands on one of our shoulders.

In *here* she undid what the uniforms were meant to do: drive us out of sight. *Here* was where she penetrated beneath the veils. *There* stood the edifice that embodied the destinies designed for us. *Here* was openness, where she taught us to think, argue, feel passionately, and be unashamed. *Here* was our common girlhood. "In addition to being the ugliest bunch, you're also the unluckiest bunch I've ever had," she often said.

Unlucky because of the times. Unlucky because we were the first generation ever to be frisked at the school gates every morning by peer volunteers who called themselves "Members of the Islamic Society," an arm of the SAVAMA, the new secret police stationed in schools. Rosy-faced students waited in line to have their cheeks rubbed to ensure their blush was natural. Girls with long eyelashes had to pull at them to prove they were real. Those with books other than school texts were interrogated, their books confiscated. Day after day, I surrendered another volume of Romain Rolland's *Jean Christophe,* another title by Jack London, a new Beatles album, to a "sister" at the door.

Mrs. Arman gave us courage to face a bitter fact: We were in exile in our own city. We were girls, living in a female ghetto. Instead of yellow armbands, we wore the sign of our inferiority on our heads. We switched sidewalks when we saw men approaching. Beaches, family parks, movie theaters had all been segregated. In the back of every bus, a sign read: SISTERS MUST SIT ONLY IN THIS AREA! And Mrs. Arman wanted us not to suffer our circumstances alone. In our misery, we had one another. And we had literature.

In late May of that year, after the conclusion of our finals, Mrs. Arman's groupies came to visit our class again. They had learned, before we had, that the thirteen-year Arman famine was at last over: she had given another nineteen to one of the composition essays written by a senior. And since Mrs. Arman thrived on stirring suspense among us, she refused to offer a hint as to who the recipient might be.

Two days before the report cards were to be handed out, I was sitting at lunch with a group of my classmates when Mrs. Arman appeared at the other end of the schoolyard. Spotting me from a distance, she flipped her finger to and fro and called, "Toothpick!"

I rose to my feet and examined her expression to see if I was in trouble. But being new to Armanology, I could not tell. With hesitant steps, I walked toward her. Her hand at her waist, she pointed to her watch, gesturing that time was short. There was no escaping her. I quickened my pace, and when I came within her reach, she lunged and grabbed my ear, pinching it, quite hard.

"Have you heard the news, Toothpick?"

"Aw! Aw! Easy, please!"

"Forget easy. Have you heard that I have given another nineteen?"

"Yes, ma'am."

"To whom?"

"To someone good?"

"You're the someone."

"Aaaw! Some encouragement this is."

"Encouragement? You have caused us both colossal trouble."

"I? How? Aw . . ."

"Everyone, school staff included, has asked to see your essay. Do you know what would happen if I gave it to them?" She did not wait for my reply. "Your scrawny ass would be hauled away to prison, that's what! The topic of the composition was war. A patriotic one-pager would have done! Instead, you ramble on about how destructive it is. A genius I've got on my hands! Writing just what the Islamic Society is looking to find, day in and day out, to do away with your breed."

Then came a light smack on the back of my neck. It felt deserved given my thoughtlessness. She continued, my ear still between her fingers: "That's the kind of writing that got me booted out of my university position, stupid, stupid, stupid Toothpick."

Her second smack, even lighter than the first, slid down and stroked my back. As if ruminating aloud, she continued: "Here's the plan: I'll tell everyone I forgot my purse with the folder of your essays in a taxi. You'll get your nineteen, and no one has to see your essay. Get it?"

"I do."

"Can you hear me, Toothpick?"

"Painfully so, ma'am."

"You're a writer."

"Pardon me?"

"You are a writer."

"As you say."

"No! You listen to me: You're a writer. I want you to say it."

"Say . . . ?"

"Say 'I'm a writer.'"

"I'm a writer."

"What are you gonna do with it?"

"Whatever you say!"

"Is your scrawny ass gonna waste it all?"

"Can talent, too, be lost that way, ma'am?"

Fury flashed in her eyes. A few silent seconds passed. "Funny is only good when the time is right. Did I not teach you anything?" And she let go of my ear.

I said, "I did not mean to—"

"Shhh!"

She reached into her purse and brought out a fountain pen. "Take this! It belonged to my father, the great Arman, the writer. Put it to better use than I have. Keep it. Something to remember these terrible days by. And promise me not to waste yourself."

Her father's pen in my hand, my head on her chest, I wanted to promise her nothing less than the world. But being a teenager, I only murmured, "Yes, ma'am!"

When school let out that day, I found myself walking toward the old neighborhood. As in years past, I was headed there in search of solace. I wanted to see Z. I needed to stand at her door and hear her shriek with joy to see me. I wanted to be where the only thing amiss was a pair of sandals on the wrong feet. With Z, I could go back in time. From her rooftop, I could climb to the rooftop of our old house. We could sit and watch the sunset together, and I would even confess that there had been no extraterrestrial friends, just a tin cover, a sinking sun, and a girl trying to make another believe in her so she could believe in herself. I wanted to dive into that basement once more and watch Great-Uncle pray. I wanted to be where every grudge was nothing the allure of a languorous afternoon could not cure. I wanted to see three o'clock undress Bibi again. No more a voyeur, I wanted to be a witness to beauty, living on.

It was a relief to see Z's door ajar as always. But I rang. No answer came. I pushed the door open and scanned the grounds. The magnolia was in bloom, but the flowerbeds were unkempt. The box shrubs had gone untrimmed. The hose with which Great-Uncle washed his hands was missing. Behind the door, in place of Z's brothers' bicycles, was a folded wheelchair. The kitchen window swung open, and a woman, looking like a much older, decimated Mrs. Banoo, shouted, "What is it?" in young Mrs. Banoo's voice.

"Excuse me." Confronted by her brusqueness, I replied in a formal tone. "I'm a friend of Z's, here to see—"

She turned away from the window and shouted again, "Z! Roya is at the door," then shut the window, without inviting me in.

Moments later, I heard footsteps echoing in the narrow hallway leading to the courtyard. They were stern and deliberate steps. In the distance, the footsteps matched a figure in a black veil. I did not recognize the person fluttering toward me, as there was so little of her face exposed to be recognized. But when she came closer, I saw the hand that was holding the veil under her chin. The hand I had never missed, not even in the lightless chest room. The hand so bony Father had likened it to the hands of starving Ethiopian children on the evening news. The hand I had pounded with my fist, pretended to cut with make-believe scissors, wrapped in my own countless times. The nails, so prim, on a girl who had always been reassuringly awry. Forget the veil, I thought, it was this hand I had come to see. Everything I yearned for was in this hand, and that it happened to be holding a veil could not possibly matter now.

"Hello, Roya!" Her sound had no veil. Its timbre was gentle as ever. "Long time, no see!"

Only her words, orderly, measured, had matured, but not the voice. Her sound. What joy it was to hear that sound again. If only I could close my eyes, conjure the girl I knew, stand still, and listen to her talk. How much more tolerable everything would be in Iran if only I could live in it blind. Live by touch, by sound, qualities that had proven much harder to alter.

"Wanna come in?" she asked, and I nodded.

She looped her veiled arm around mine as we crossed the courtyard. On the second floor, a hand struggled to grasp the handle of the windows but faltered. When the window finally swung open, a face, peeking above the sill, mumbled a few unintelligible words. Z saw that I was puzzled: "Reza is saying hello!"

"Which Reza?"

"Reza, my brother."

"Your Reza? No."

"He's the only survivor of an infantry that was ambushed in a border town six months ago. The right side of his body is paralyzed."

"Up there? That is Reza?"

"The slurring is supposed to go away in a few months."

I smiled at the creature who had steadied his torso on a set of trembling elbows. Reza: the indispensable Sabbath visitor to our observing household who turned the lights off late on Friday evenings and showed up every Saturday before noon to turn on the stove without our asking him. Reza: Father's honorary fourth son, the only one willing to accompany him on chores the real Hakakian children never would—car washing or grocery shopping. Reza: the "Spaceship *Enterprise*" of the Alley of the Distinguished, who rocketed himself through the first-floor windows and landed in his spot across from Father at the backgammon set, always playing the white pieces. That Reza was greeting me.

I stood transfixed, until Z took charge and promised to bring me up to him for a few minutes before I left. Then we linked arms again as she ushered me down the stairs to the basement.

"How long have you been wearing a black veil, Z?" I asked. We climbed on top of the chest, on the peak of our childhood, the space of our unabashed curiosities.

She whispered, "Only on days I go to visit Bibi."

"Bibi! How is she? Where is she?"

She paused, stood up to take off her veil and scarf. I took off my scarf, too. And doing so, we peeled away the years to become "us" again, only a bit taller, plumper. We repositioned ourselves on the chest. But Z was strangely somber.

"Tell me," I asked again. "Bibi has been on my mind so much lately."

She brought her face so close I felt the tip of her nose against my ear. At that distance, we could never keep any secret from each other. "Bibi is in prison," she breathed, and went on to tell me the rest.

Bibi had joined the People's Mujahideen, the largest armed opposition organization, a few months after the revolution. Sometime in 1982 when the organization was banned, she had written a fiery essay condemning the ban and read it before her class during a composition hour. The next day, an Islamic Society turncoat in her class reported her. With an already hefty file on her, the Society found the essay to be the last damning piece of evidence of Bibi's "anti-revolutionary activities." Two uniformed guards, accompanied by the principal, had escorted Bibi out of the classroom, shoved her into one of their Toyota SUVs, and driven off.

I clasped my arms around my knees and curled myself on the chest. Z put her hands on my back and spoke, as a quiet, steady stream of tears dripped off my chin and onto her jeans.

Bibi's arrest was only the beginning of the grim events that were to follow. A few months later, Great-Uncle, broken by a guilty conscience for having led his niece into politics, died of a heart attack. A month later, Mrs. Banoo suffered her breakdown.

Z talked, no longer waiting for me to ask questions. The once-fidgety girl spoke softly, decorously, for as long as she felt my shoulders shake to sobs under her hands. After her uncle's death, Mrs. Banoo went to visit Bibi in prison. She wanted to break the news about Great-Uncle to Bibi in person. In the visiting room, mother and daughter were about to embrace when Mrs. Banoo spotted on Bibi's bare elbow, extended from under the veil, a strange purplish mark. She drew the arm to her to examine it closely. Bibi twisted her body to wrest her elbow free from her mother's grip. The mark looked like a triangle, with its base missing. Each of its two sides was a fluid-filled blister. The sides were cherry red at the outer edges and pink toward the middle. Mrs. Banoo rolled Bibi's sleeve higher, where she found another mark. The size had not changed, but the tip, where the two lines converged, pointed to Bibi's armpit, as if a scalding object had skidded along her daughter's arm. And then it dawned on her: Bibi had been branded by a hot instrument. The tip of a press iron, perhaps. "How did this happen to you?" Mrs. Banoo pleaded with her daughter. But Bibi would not look her mother in the eye, nor would she answer. The guards warned Mrs. Banoo to stop asking questions or she would have to leave. Bibi's avoidance, coupled with the guards' warnings, made clear to Mrs. Banoo how the marks had been inflicted on Bibi. And what was a mother to do for a wounded child? She hurled herself at Bibi and dragged her to the door, roaring at the guards. They intervened, whisked Bibi off her mother's embrace and back to the cell. Then came a shriek. Mrs. Banoo fainted. The next day she was hospitalized in a psychiatric ward.

Z, so much tougher than her looks had let on, held my head in her lap until I finally asked, "What can we do for her?"

"Nothing, really."

"Maybe we can buy her something. A gift. Anything at all."

"No guarantee she will get it. Visits are rarely granted."

"I'll bring my old copy of *The Little Black Fish*. It'll remind her of the good days."

"Oh no! That would upset her even more."

"You're wrong. She loved that book. She loved Samad Behrangi."

On Z's lips a sad smile formed. Her gaze drifted across my face. Her finger traced a line around my ear. For the first time in all the years I had known her, she treated me like a parent trying to introduce adult realities to a sunny child: "It's not the book, but what she learned in prison that would upset her even more."

"What did she learn in prison?"

Samad Behrangi had not been drowned. There had been no cement blocks. No cruel intervention by SAVAK. A poor swimmer, he had drowned on his own. When news of the drowning reached several leading anti-shah intellectuals of the time, they saw it as an opportunity to pin it on the shah to fuel the public's resentment of him. One of the pivotal legends that had tormented a generation and ignited the revolution had been nothing but a hoax. A strategic maneuver! A little lie between revolutionary friends! What of it?

I meant to tell Z what she was saying was unbelievable. But instead I blurted, "What are you saying?"

And she repeated the story once more.

"What are you saying, Z?" My lips moved to those words yet again. This time, she knew better than to repeat herself.

In four years, Z had lost an uncle to grief, a brother to war, a sister to prison, and a mother to insanity. And there I was, a helpless pet, cooing to her to explain the inexplicable. Once her weaknesses, mirroring my own, had bonded us. Now her great share of despair was driving us apart. It made a giant of her, while I was still a girl and frail.

"You're lucky, Roya," Z murmured, for at that moment, "luck" seemed the only lesson in all the dark tales she had told me.

"You're a Jew. Once you leave Iran, you'll get a visa to any country in the world. But where can I go?"

"But I don't want to go anywhere else," I said, though I knew my objection made me no less lucky in her eyes.

"You must go," she continued. "Go soon! Leave and never look back."

I said good-bye to Z in a blur. On the way home, I could not feel my feet hitting the ground. The cars passed in a blur. I felt lost, not in the city but inside my clothes. Under my uniform, I was a blur. Where had Roya gone? I stopped, opened the top buttons of my uniform, and peeked inside: *Where am I?* I saw only darkness. A cave that led to a pair of denim cuffs, faded blue suede shoes, and dirty asphalt. Somewhere under that musty blackness I was hidden. What wafted out of my eighteen-year-old collar was nothing exuberant or redolent of girlhood, but an eighteen-hundred-year-old stench of something gone bad. Very bad. And I realized that something was a girl gone bad. *I* had gone bad. The lies had festered in me. The lies I had been told about everything. The lies I had told to others. Maybe the festering had begun before me, Samad Behrangi, the shah, or Khomeini, and I was simply born into it. Maybe it had all begun with the great Hafez, with his hyperbolic loves, with his celebration of blind sacrifice, with his shadowy muses, and his wordplay that should never have become guidebook of the nation.

I grabbed the two corners of my collar, brought them to my ears, and wept. How heavy it had become. Each side felt like a stiff mold, my scarf cement around my head. Would it ever come off? Could it? Or was I trapped in it for good? I saw no sign of myself under the hardened shrouds. My body had atrophied. Bibi had been visible. Her gleaming body, beauty blinding. And I was the one fading. Only I, equally guilty, equally innocent, walked free, yet I felt lost. I, who read what Bibi had read, wrote essays like she had written, slid past the guard or, if detained, got away every time. My talent was not writing. My talent was deception. Such great aspirations, and all I had become was a masterful liar. Through this inferno, I had charted a crafty path, disguising myself as a traveler:

Excuse me, brother, but you don't want to arrest me. What would I have to do with politics? You see, I am a Jew. Allow me to spell it: capital S, p, i, n, e, and then "less," as in "without." My mother, father, brothers, and all of our ancestors are Jews. Generation after generation of cowards. Yes, brother. Only money is on our minds. Gold, to be exact. In this slow market silver, too. Yes, sister. Arresting me would be a waste of your precious time. This book you see in my bag, some Muslim classmate gave me. Otherwise what would the likes of me have to do with Maxim Gorky? John Steinbeck? Never heard of him. George Orwell? Psssh. You look at me: Do I look like someone who gives a damn? Was it not your beautiful handwriting on the wall across our door, "Johouds Go Home"? My real homeland is Israel. True, I wasn't born there, went there as a child once, can't carry on a conversation in Hebrew, don't write in it, or speak it with my family. Still, sister, for me there's only Israel. Allow me to correct that: I mean the Occupied Palestine. The place where you warn I should flee to, but then you plan to wrest it free from the clutches of the bloodsucking Zionists. But not to worry, brother! Your paradoxical advice is lost on me. Any ambiguity uttered by you reaches me better than bolts of divine lightning and naturally are perfectly enlightening. Allahu-Akbar! May I go now?

Come catch me, you bastards! I have done it, too. These were my last thoughts before I was startled by the sound of an explosion. I looked up to see where it had come from. Across the street, at the eastern corner of Farahbakhsh Square, stood a member of the Revolutionary Guard with a rocket-propelled grenade launcher on his shoulder. Behind him, a few others huddled. Had they come for me at last? One of them was looking in my direction. Had Bibi's home been under surveillance? Several more armed men were cordoning off the sidewalk. Should I simply rush the inevitable, walk over to them and turn myself in? Even *my* luck had to run out. I had to be next: The next to be arrested. The next to be tortured or executed. The next to flee. Sooner rather than later, something would crush everything: An Iraqi bomb. A raid by the Revolutionary Guards. An outlawed book. A forbidden song. The wrong sentence in a school essay. Anyone could be an agent of SAVAMA, a brainwashed zealot wanting to serve Allah by serving the imam: The old woman in the floral-print veil limping away. The ogling teenage boy on the stoop. The blind man walking without a cane. Somewhere along the way, no matter where I was going, there was always a checkpoint. Somewhere behind, someone always followed. Nothing was predictable. Gone were the ordinary days, the soothing rhythm of perfunctory chores, the serenity of boredom. *Come find me, monotony!* Routines were only a memory. Time no longer simply passed. It became a countdown. *There is no getting away. Turn yourself in!*

From the guards' vehicles came the sound of the Koran. They had come to seize another safe house, a leftist cell, or an opposition group's headquarters. All parties had been banned, except for Hezbollah, the Party of God.

Tears were running down my cheeks, which would make me look like a sympathizer of the safe house, in whose vicinity a single lapse, a slight show of emotion, was clear guilt by association. Surely I appeared suspicious to the two men who were eyeing the trespassers from the other corner. Sadness would be incriminating. I had to think quickly of an excuse for my tears. A guard had spotted me. Turning away was impossible now. Others behind him were exchanging fire with guerilla fighters inside the apartment building. Two guards were scaling the building. One was commanding them from the rooftop.

The guard motioned to me as he held a rag in front of his face. I could feel my feet at last, and they were leaden. I held my breath, hoping it would stop the tears. But before I reached him, he shouted, "Sister, don't come this way! The brothers just teargassed the area."

Tear gas! That old, faithful alibi. I let go of my breath.

Night had fallen by the time I reached our block. The power was out again. Moonlight spread along the street. The neighborhood was hushed, the way my old neighborhood had once been, preparing itself for nine o'clock, for the moment of protest. Then, too, electricity was off and nothing lit the area but the moon. I looked at the sky. It was the ravishing moon, the shifting ink blots of shadows on its face, that had deceived us. No! Not deceived, *bewitched* was what it had done. This darkness had patterned itself after the night: it fell not suddenly but in stages. Our 1979 sky had not borrowed its glory from a breaking dawn. It had been a sky at dusk. From then on, black had encroached in variations of gray. And our eyes justified each new gradation, until blackness had fallen. If anything had to be banished from Iran, it was the moon. Dismantle it! Full, half, crescent, down to the last of its capricious operations. We should have never mapped our destinies on earth by reading the face of a heavenly body. Rain should have been all the meddling we ever wished from above.

At home, Mother was working in the kitchen by the light of a kerosene lantern. Her face brightened with relief when she saw me at the door. "Where's Father?" I asked.

But Mother only said, "Sit down. Have some dinner first."

First? My mind was already on that ominous "second." I left the kitchen to look for Father. He was not in the living room. The radio was on in his bedroom, so he could not have gone too far. The bathroom door was open. Mother was trailing me, quietly pleading under her breath, "You know we love you. All we have is you. All we want is your well-being."

Each sentence only heightened my foreboding. In Father's study, a candle was burning. I turned back and headed to my own bedroom. But my own door was locked. "Where is Father?" I shot at Mother.

Standing at my bedroom door, I could hear feet shuffling inside at some distance, far enough to be on the balcony.

"He had to," Mother said, "for your own safety."

I knocked hard on the door. With each knock, the feet picked up speed. They moved methodically: paced a few steps, stopped for a few seconds. Then came a *thud!* And the feet moved again.

"What's happening?" I fired at Mother once more.

But a barely audible "Don't be upset" was her reply.

Another *thud!* I knocked harder and called out to Father. The feet moved much faster, followed by a few consecutive thuds and crackles. Then silence fell. The feet shuffled no more. The key turned on the other side. I quickly pressed the handle. The door opened to Father, on the other side, his face covered in sweat and ash. His clothes were rumpled, his demeanor that of a prizefighter, thoroughly trampled. The room had a guilty air. My eyes scanned every corner. A band of moonlight had fallen aslant on my bed. Strangely, it was unmade. The mattress under which I hid magazines and other personal things had been moved. The box of my notebooks usually stowed under the bed was in the middle of the room, empty.

Father held a long wooden stick charred at one end. He moved away from the door and leaned against my bookshelf. Mother stepped in and stood by him. I lingered at the door, as if to step inside would make me an accomplice in the wrong the room reeked of. Scanning the surroundings once again, I paused at the bookshelves. Tracing the direction of my look, my parents huddled closer to each other. "Move, Mother!" Because she was ever the easier parent to overcome, I called to her. But she did not move and only turned to Father.

"Father, please!" I shouted.

They stepped aside to give me a view of my bookshelves: empty! Ten previously overstuffed rows now contained only a set of dictionaries, a copy of the Old Testament, and the collected poetry of Hafez. I smelled plastic burning. On the balcony, my eye caught the flicker of a dying fire. Mother implored again: "Don't be upset, please. They were unsafe to keep at home."

Among the ashes, in the bonfire, my world was burning: my newspapers and magazines, my fifth-grade appreciation certificate from the shah's minister of education. Underneath them, my weightier loves had settled: Albert's copy of *The Little Black Fish,* my records and tapes, signed copies of my favorite poetry books, my *Jane Austen Reader,* my hardcover Mikhail Sholokhov's *And Quiet Flows the Don,* my leather-bound Dostoyevskys—all burning to punish me for what should never have been a crime.

I knelt before the heap and leaned into the fire to discover the first layer of kindling: my diary, my own book of poems, now only identifiable by their thick spines that had yet to burn.

Father walked onto the balcony. He stood behind me, lay both hands on my shoulders, cleared his throat, and said faintly, "It's time we leave for America."

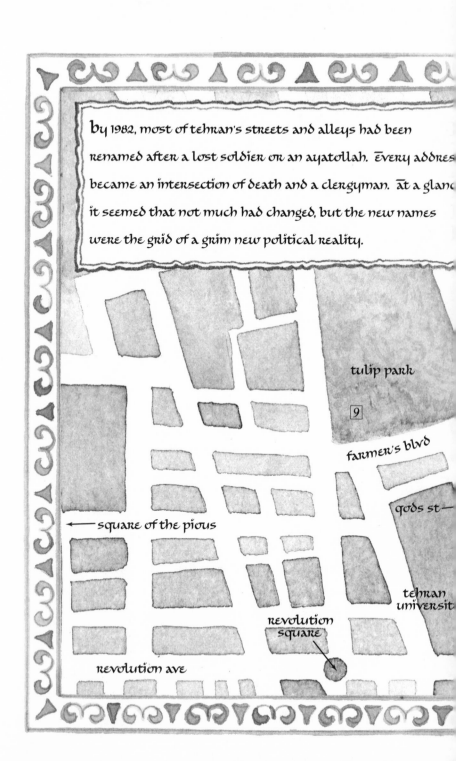

by 1982, most of tehran's streets and alleys had been renamed after a lost soldier or an ayatollah. every addres[s] became an intersection of death and a clergyman. at a glan[ce] it seemed that not much had changed, but the new names were the grid of a grim new political reality.

tulip park

9

farmer's blvd

qods st—

square of the pious

tehran universit[y]

revolution square

revolution ave

tehran 1984

1 Victoria Hotel

2 Qods Cinema

3 Abandoned building

4 Mostaz'afeen Foundation

5 The Music Shop

6 Negeen Confectioners

7 City Theater

8 Embassy of Palestine

9 Museum

10 "Do Nike" fast food eatery

11 The Martyr Motahari College Preparatory Institute for Boys

12 The Friday Prayer Coordination Center

1

2

messiah square

alley of the distinguished

minoo alley

3

st of martyr mozaffari brothers

10

4

5

6

11

damascus st

12

palestine square

ayatollah talegani ave

7

8

messiah park

palestine ave

messiah ave

hafez st

EPILOGUE

IN THE EARLY 1990S, NUMBER THREE ALLEY OF THE DISTIN-
guished was demolished. The architect who designed the replacement was surely a butcher: the junipers were chopped off
and the courtyard was leveled. A hideous, poorly maintained
edifice replaced our home. Since the city's explosive growth, the
Crown Prince Square area no longer falls within the trendy ter-
ritories of Tehran. Yet the alley's name remains the same.

A friend traveling to Iran last year visited the old neighborhood on my behalf. Z was still living in the same house, where
she raises her children. There were no signs of Bibi. Z said little
to our intermediary but jotted down my mailing address and
promised to send a letter. No letter ever came.

The school from which I had been excused in the afternoons is among the handful of remaining Hebrew schools of Tehran. However, Raah-e Danesh School did not survive Mrs. Moghadam's grand ambitions. It was taken over and turned into a boys' elementary school called Martyr Mostafa Khomeini's School. Even Mrs. Moghadam herself did not survive her own grand ambitions. Running for a seat in the Majles, she died in a bus crash on the campaign trail.

Uncle Ardi has lived in Israel ever since. He married an Israeli woman, has three daughters, and does without luxuries like a BMW. Accompanied by a girlfriend, I visited him at his beachfront Netanya home in May 2002. By the time dinner was over, my twenty-four-year-old companion had developed a catastrophic crush on Uncle Ardi. Fortunately, we left the country the next day.

Grandmother died in Los Angeles in 1997 but passed her best recipes to Mother before she did. Aunt Zarrin took her last car ride with Jahan on Queens Boulevard in New York, where their car collided with a truck. He was unscathed. She died instantly. Years later, with three children in tow, Farah finally got a divorce. Uncle A.J. and his sons support her on the income from their jewelry booths in downtown Los Angeles.

The Jewish Iranian Students Organization moved from Pride Street to a new location. Though the membership has plummeted to fewer than one hundred, the hiking committee still meets at 5:00 A.M. at the foot of the Alborz every Friday morning.

Nazila is happily married and settled in the San Fernando Valley with her husband and two daughters. Mrs. Ferdows has an apartment in the vicinity and has learned to respect the laws against noise pollution in the new country. Most of the old dreamers live in Los Angeles. The perfect proof of Mrs. Ferdows's warning to never put boys next to girls is this: Nearly all the dreamers married each other. In each other, they found the only remembrance of their irretrievable past. They dream little now and reminisce instead. They do not climb mountains, only occasionally gather and let their children play together. Most of them make their livelihood as fashion retailers in south Los Angeles. Only Roya Jr. and Eddie live in Israel. Of the group, two remain in Tehran, where, disguising their Jewish identities, they run one of the city's most successful art establishments.

The last I heard of Mrs. Arman was in 1987, after Father paid her a visit before his departure. She sent her love and a few books of poetry. She was contemplating retirement.

Tofigh was never published again. Several other publications have since tried to emulate it, but none capture the humor of the original.

When I was walking past the row of Iranian bookstores on Westwood Boulevard in Los Angeles several months ago, I asked a shopkeeper if he had a copy of *The Little Black Fish.* Of the two men managing the store, the younger did not know the book, and the older, startled by my question, said admonishingly, "*The Little Black Fish*? Missus, do you not know the era of Samad Behrangi is long over and that case is altogether obsolete nowadays? Go on, now! Go get on with your life."

Agha died in 1989, without my intervention, simply of old age. When the helicopter lifted his coffin, his corpse slid and fell on top of the mourners. That was the last record of his heavenly presence in the sky. No other mortal face has been traced in Iran's moon since 1979.

"Allahu-Akbar" is an unpopular chant, heard only in mosques or at rallies of radical Muslims. The young generation expresses its enthusiasm by simply clapping in applause.

Reverend Jerry Cochran's diagnosis was declared "dust-induced lung disease," and his story aired on *60 Minutes II*. He received Congressional Recognition in 2000 for his work on his own behalf and that of his fellow servicemen, and was appointed to the Minority Veterans' Affairs Committee by the U.S. Congress to look at minority issues in the navy.

Albert, Javid, and Bez are married and scattered over the East Coast of the United States. Mother has far less to worry about but worries nonetheless. She attends English classes at a Jewish center in Queens and keeps remarkably active. Father's eyes are not so good now, but that has only slightly lessened the traffic of the glasses between his forehead and the bridge of his nose. His poetry airs regularly on exile radio stations, and he contributes to several expatriate magazines. He refuses to travel and insists that the only place worth visiting is his native village, Khonsar, where not a single Jew remains.

David and I still write each other, though the subjects of our correspondence have since surpassed Iran. In four years, his poetic skills have improved significantly, while I have learned to write using fewer metaphors.

And I am the lucky one, *escaped only to tell thee*. What more it took is a story I must leave for another time.

GLOSSARY OF TERMS

ABA: *(Arabic)* A loose-fitting outer garment worn primarily by Muslim clergymen.

AGHA: *(Persian)* A term of reverence both for an ordinary male and for one leading a family or religious order.

ALLAHU–AKBAR: *(Arabic)* God is Great. It became an important antishah chant during the months of the revolution and replaced the ordinary applause, by clapping of hands, in postrevolutionary Iran.

ASHOURA: *(Arabic)* The tenth. As an occasion, it refers to the tenth day of the month of Moharram in the Arab calendar, believed to be the day on which the third Shiite imam, Imam Hussein, was martyred in A.D. 680.

BARBARI: A type of bread.

BISM ALLAH AL-RAHMAN AL-RAHIM: *(Arabic)* In the name of God the compassionate the merciful. It is the Arabic equivalent of "In the name of God."

DHALEK AL KETAB O LA RAY BA FEE: *(Arabic)* The opening line of the Cow Chapter in the Koran, meaning, "There is no untruth in this book."

FATWA: *(Arabic)* Edict.

HAJI: *(Arabic)* Pilgrim. Originally used to refer to a person who had made a pilgrimage to Mecca, but in colloquial Persian, it is also a term of reverence.

HEZBOLLAH: *(Arabic)* Party of God.

IMAM ALI: *(Persian)* The first of the twelve Shiite imams.

INSHALLAH: *(Arabic)* God willing.

IST: *(Persian)* Stop!

JAVEED SHAH: *(Persian)* Long live the shah.

LA-ELA-HA-EL-ALLAH: *(Arabic)* There is no other God except Allah. In colloquial Persian, it is also uttered by a frustrated person who wishes not to be indignant.

MAJLES: *(Arabic)* A place of gathering. It is also Persian for the National Assembly.

MASHALLAH: *(Arabic)* As God wishes. A term of encouragement or admiration by which someone prays that God protect the admired person or object from the "evil eye."

MOSTAZ'AFEEN: *(Arabic)* The powerless, the downtrodden. The term was popularized by Ayatollah Khomeini as the radical Islamic counterpart to the communist proletariat.

NAJES: *(Arabic)* Unholy, unclean.

SALAVAT: *(Arabic)* An invitation to the traditional Muslim utterance of salute upon prophet Muhammad and all his kin.

SANGAK: A type of bread.

SAVAK: *(Persian)* An acronym standing for the shah's secret intelligence service.

SAVAMA: *(Persian)* Also an acronym, standing for the much humbler predecessor, SAVAMA refers to the vast and highly sophisticated operations that is the Intelligence Ministry in postrevolutionary Iran.

SHAH: *(Persian)* King.

SOFREH: *(Persian)* A cloth spread on the floor around which meals are eaten.

TAFTOON: A type of bread.

YA ALI: *(Arabic)* May Imam Ali help us!

CHRONOLOGY

530 B.C.E.

The arrival of Jews in Persia following the fall of Jerusalem.

A.D. 642

The Arab conquest of Persia.

1906

Introduction of constitution limits the royal absolutism of the past dynasties that ruled over Persia for centuries. The first national assembly, Majles, is established, in which Ayatollah Behbahani, a Muslim cleric, represents the Jews.

1917

The October Revolution takes place in Russia, Persia's northern neighbor.

1925

The Qajar dynasty is abolished and the reign of the Pahlavi dynasty begins.

1935

Iran replaces Persia as the official name of the country.

1936

Reza Shah Pahlavi bans women from appearing in public with headdress or veil.

1941

Mohammad Reza Shah Pahlavi assumes power.

1950

Haghnazar Hakakian goes to Tehran to attend university.

1951

The Majles votes to nationalize the oil industry and elects Prime Minister Muhammad Mosadegh to implement and oversee the nationalization. This leads to a British boycott of Iranian oil. A power struggle between the shah and the prime minister ensues.

1953

With the backing of the United States, Great Britain, and several powerful Iranian religious leaders, a coup d'état is staged, which topples the Mosadegh government.

Haghnazar meets his wife-to-be, Helen, at a teacher education seminar in Tehran.

1954

Helen and Haghnazar marry.

1962

Iranian women are granted the right to vote.

1963

Through the "White Revolution" the shah implements programs for land reform and modernization in Iran.

1964

Ayatollah Khomeini is sent into exile.

1966

Roya Hakakian is born.

1967

The Hakakians move to number three Alley of the Distinguished.

1968

Samad Behrangi, the renowned schoolteacher and writer of children's stories, dies.

1975

Albert Hakakian goes to the United States.

1977

The "Ten Nights of Poetry" at the Goethe Institute in Tehran is staged to demand the end of censorship.

1978

The strike of the oil workers, which paralyzes Iran's economy, begins.

Javid and Behzad Hakakian go to the United States.

January 1979

The shah leaves Iran.

February 1979

Ayatollah Khomeini returns to Iran and assumes power.

The Family Protection Law is reversed, lifting the restriction on polygamy and giving men full rights in divorce and custody. The marriage age for girls is lowered to nine.

Ayatollah Khomeini appoints a provisional government headed by Mehdi Bazargan and other politically moderate ministers.

March 1979

Women are banned from serving as judges. Beaches and sports events are segregated by sex. Ayatollah Khomeini issues an edict ordering women to appear in Islamic uniform in the workplace, but after a major demonstration against it, he backs down.

April 1979

In a national referendum the overwhelming majority of Iranians choose an Islamic Republic as their form of government.

Habib Elghanian, Iran's leading Jewish philanthropist, is executed.

Number three Alley of the Distinguished is sold.

October 1979

The shah is admitted to the United States for medical treatment.

November 1979

The U.S. embassy in Tehran is seized and fifty-two Americans are held hostage. Subsequently, the provisional government of Mehdi Bazargan collapses. A new, more hardline government is appointed.

June 1980

Ayatollah Khomeini declares the "administrative revolution" requiring women to wear Islamic uniform in all government offices.

Universities are shut down to undergo "cultural revolution."

August 1980

Ayatollah Khomeini appoints six clergymen to the twelve-member Council of Guardians of the Constitution, to examine all parliamentary decisions for their consistency with the tenets of Islam. The council gets veto power over laws ratified by the Majles.

September 1980

Iraqi forces invade Iran and a war, lasting for nearly a decade, ensues.

January 1981

Ronald Reagan's inauguration coincides with the release of the American hostages in Tehran.

September 1982

Universities reopen.

All public schools are ordered segregated by gender.

1983

The Islamic penal code is implemented. Under this law, women who do not abide by the Islamic dress code must receive seventy-four lashes, and those who commit adultery must be stoned to death.

August 1984

Helen and Roya leave Iran.

May 1985

Helen and Roya arrive in New York.

1987

Haghnazar leaves Iran.

1988

The war with Iraq ends.

Ayatollah Khomeini issues a fatwa calling for the death of Salman Rushdie.

Haghnazar arrives in the United States.

June 1989

Ayatollah Khomeini dies.

1997

Mohammad Khatami wins the presidential elections in a landslide victory.

July 1999

"Tiananmen of Iran," the largest student uprisings since 1979, occurs.

ACKNOWLEDGMENTS

To write a book about Iran in English became a reality on a blistering August noon over pasta. David introduced me to Verlyn Klinkenborg, who gave me all of his best lessons at that lunch and encouraged me to contact his agent. That agent, Flip Brophy, and I met on February 14, 2001, and as it was destined, our encounter was love at first sight. Flip took the book to Annik La Farge, a gutsy editor who was willing to gamble on a little-known immigrant writer. I am grateful to this cast, without whom my book would never be.

And without Cora Weiss and Wade Greene, the writer would never be. So goes for Pierre Schori, the patron saint of stranded journalists in hostile airports, and his passionate and principled Maud; also for Olara Otunnu, who insisted that I dare to write, and do so in English; and to Jill Cutler, who read my manuscript with remarkable diligence and enriched it with her insights.

While I worked, delving into bitter memories, a few friends sweetened my hours: Jeremy Brecher and his Yelping Hill community; Mark and Amy Atkinson, who have always put their faith in me; the generous Lucia Stern, the keen Susan Brown, and the angelic Karen Cera, whose packages kept on arriving when I was at the MacDowell Colony. The Colony has since become this pilgrim's Plymouth Rock and her Wailing Wall together on the same tender stretch of land.

I also thank Crown Publishers' Camille Smith, tolerator-in-chief of the Hakakian mess, the amazing Meg Drislane, Ahmad Ashraf at *Encyclopedia Iranica* and his Azar at the Princeton University Library for guiding me through the research; Kamran Broukhim and Ouriel Karamat for providing me with the accounts of the postrevolutionary tumults in the Jewish community as experienced by its leaders; Jahanshah Javid for his indispensable Iranian.com; Ali Sajjadi for his friendship and his treasure trove of newspaper archives; my two brilliant coconspirators—the composer Jamshied Sharifi and the painter Niki Nodjoumi—who have never said no to a collaboration with me; and the unrivaled Elham Gheytanchi, who has mothered my poetry through the years. And most thanks to my unrelenting critic and supplier of all great music and literature Abdee Kalantari.

Lastly, I am grateful to my family, especially to my parents, who have so easily loved a most difficult child. And to Ramin, the gentlest, most magnanimous partner a girl could ever have.

ABOUT THE AUTHOR

ROYA HAKAKIAN is a former associate producer at CBS's *60 Minutes* and a documentary filmmaker. She is the author of two acclaimed volumes of poetry in Persian and a recipient of the 2002–2003 Dewitt Wallace–Reader's Digest Fellowship. She lives in Connecticut.